Pragmatism, Rights, and Democracy

AMERICAN PHILOSOPHY SERIES

Pragmatism, Rights, and Democracy

BETH J. SINGER

FORDHAM UNIVERSITY PRESS
New York
1999

LC 98–23028
ISBN 0–8232–1867–8 (*hardcover*)
ISBN 0–8232–1868–6 (*paperback*)
ISSN 1073–2764
American Philosophy Series, No. 11
Vincent M. Colapietro, Editor
Vincent G. Potter (1929–1994), Founding Editor

Library of Congress Cataloging-in-Publication Data

Singer, Beth J., 1927–
    Pragmatism, rights, and democracy / Beth J. Singer.
        p.   cm. — (American philosophy series : no. 11)
    Includes bibliographical references and index.
    ISBN 0–8232–1867–8 (hardcover). — ISBN 0–8232–1868–6 (pbk.)
    1. Human rights.   2. Community.   3. Individualism.
    4. Pragmatism.   I. Title.   II. Series
JC571.S6285   1999
323′.01—dc21   98–23028
                                                                                    CIP

Printed in the United States of America

To my colleagues and students
in the
Brooklyn College Philosophy Department

CONTENTS

ACKNOWLEDGMENTS

Chapter 4, "The Democratic Solution to Ethnic Pluralism," first appeared in *Philosophy and Social Criticism*, 19, No. 2 (1993). It is reprinted here by permission of Sage Publications, Inc.

I am indebted to many people for their assistance in preparing this volume. I am especially grateful to the following for their critical reading of drafts of the various chapters: György Andrássy, Katy Gray Brown, Gary Calore, Vincent Colapietro, Daniel Dombrowski, Frederic R. Kellogg, John Lachs, Thelma Z. Lavine, Shepard Liu, Martin Matustik, Justyna Miklaszewska, David M. Rasmussen, John Ryder, and Kenneth W. Stikkers. I also want to express my gratitude to Abraham Edel, Susan Haack, Peter H. Hare, George L. Kline, Henry Rosemont, Jr., John E. Smith, and Marilyn Smith who, over the years, have read and commented on my work and helped me develop the ideas presented here.

I also want to express my appreciation to Vincent Colapietro for the encouragement and moral support he has given me in his capacity as Editor of the Fordham University Press American Philosophy Series. My thanks as well to Rick Repetti for proofreading and Jody Larson for preparing the index; and I must thank Mary Beatrice Schulte, Executive Editor at the Press.

PREFACE

Composed, for the most part, as separate papers, the chapters of this book can all be read independently. They are unified, however, by the fact that in each of them I attempt to develop implications of the theory of rights presented in my book *Operative Rights*.[1] Originally written for different audiences, most of whose members could not be expected to be familiar with the content of that book, the chapters necessarily contain some repetition, although in editing them for publication I have endeavored to eliminate some of this. But partly in response to comments from others—readers and reviewers of the book as well as those who commented on and contributed to discussion of papers I presented at conferences and in lectures at universities in this country and abroad—and partly as a result of my own attempts to articulate my position more clearly, I have been compelled to rethink and reformulate certain statements that I made earlier. Therefore, some of the recurrent explanations of my central concepts aim at further clarification. In addition, in its application of the principles and theses I had enunciated there, the collection as a whole goes beyond *Operative Rights* and in so doing should serve to amplify as well as clarify my position in that work.

In Part I of the present volume, Chapter 1 is devoted to critical analysis of what I take to be widespread, central features of traditional and contemporary theories of rights as well as criticisms of those theories. In Chapter 2, I introduce my own, alternative theory, and Chapter 3 is a discussion of three modern philosophers whose views run counter to the established tradition of "natural rights" theories. In Parts II and III, I apply the principles of my own theory to pressing issues in social and political philosophy today, including the question of minority rights and problems of social conflict, ethnic conflict in particular. In Chapter 8, after discussing the views of John Dewey and George Herbert Mead concerning rights and the democratic process, I show some of the relations between my own view and theirs.

Throughout the book, a central role is assigned to the concept of community, construed as the indispensable context and condition of individuality and identity as well as rights. Understanding the mutual interdependence of identity and community, on the one hand, and the way those rights that I contend ought to be operative for all members of all communities serve to protect the integrity of those communities, on the other, should help to resolve the current conflict between communitarianism and individualistic liberalism. Analyzed in terms of shared perspectives and the development of social norms, the same concept of community is designed also to serve as the basis for an effective theory and methodology of conflict resolution. The theoretical perspective at work in this book incorporates elements of other philosophies, and Pragmatism itself is notably diversified, but in view of the centrality to my own thought of George Herbert Mead and John Dewey, I consider myself to belong to the Pragmatist tradition.

NOTE

1. Beth J. Singer, *Operative Rights* (Albany: State University of New York Press, 1993).

I

ORTHODOXY AND HETERODOXY IN THE THEORY OF RIGHTS

1

Four Principles of Traditional Theories of Rights

EVEN AS HUMAN RIGHTS come under attack in one part of the globe after another, various bodies, from the United Nations and the Organization of African Unity to the World Federation of Modern Language Associations, are trying to extend the protection afforded by rights to peoples, to families, to homosexuals, to children—even to nonhuman animals and the environment—and also to widen the scope of rights to cover such diverse entitlements as those to education and health care, to one's inherited language, culture, and religion, to personal privacy and control over one's own body (including the right to an abortion), and to death at a time and in the manner of one's own choosing. Concurrently, especially in the United States, the concept of rights is being subjected to intensive scrutiny, and new understandings of the nature and ground of rights are emerging. In this chapter I shall discuss several features of traditional theories of rights and some of the ways in which these have been challenged, both recently and in the past. I shall use the term 'rights' in a broad sense to include "human" or moral rights as well as legal rights. I shall use the word 'community' as a generic name for all groupings or associations of human beings.

Contemporary rights theory has three main sources: (1) the Christian tradition of natural law; (2) the Enlightenment theorists Hugo Grotius, Thomas Hobbes, John Locke, and Immanuel Kant; and (3) the American legal theorist Wesley N. Hohfeld. Theories in this tradition assert or assume, *inter alia*, the following interrelated principles (the names, which are necessarily somewhat arbitrary, are my own): Individualism; A priorism; Essentialism; Adversarialism. I shall discuss these in turn, together with some criticisms that have been made of them and a few contrasting views.

INDIVIDUALISM

A basic thesis of the theories I am talking about is that only individuals can have rights. Originally associated with the concept of personhood, this thesis is frequently grounded by contemporary writers in the idea that only individuals are capable of action. Alan Gewirth, a prominent theorist in the United States today, speaks of rights as "normatively necessary, personally oriented, moral requirements."[1] For some writers in the field, the view that only individuals can have rights is a metaphysical issue. Consistent with a now-outmoded school of thought in sociology, even some who assert the rights of social groups or communities deny their ontological reality. Under the influence of this view, a corporation is treated under the law as an "artificial person," and some writers speak of other kinds of community in similar terms. Lon Fuller, acknowledging that social collectivities are treated as unities and are held to have both rights and duties, nevertheless denies that they are real, calling them "legal fictions."[2] John Rawls, speaking of justice or right, says that "a conception of right is a set of principles . . . [including basic rights and duties] . . . that is to be publicly recognized as a final court of appeal for ordering the conflicting claims of *moral persons*." To allow for group rights, Rawls widens the category of moral persons to include social collectivities. He describes the social order in which the principles that assign basic rights and duties have their sphere of operation (Hegel's "civil society," which Rawls terms "private society") as comprising "persons . . . whether they are human individuals or associations."[3]

Many rights-theories are individualist in another sense, asserting the moral primacy of individual interests and individual good in determining the nature and function of rights. As Loren Lomasky states in his book *Persons, Rights, and the Moral Community,*

> Concern for basic rights is concern for the individualism they express. . . . A doctrine of basic rights . . . is . . . committed to regarding individualism as of paramount importance such that other ends taken to be of value to particular individuals or to society may not be pursued in ways that violate rights. . . . It is therefore a crucial task of the rights theorist to explain how it can be reasonable to place such a premium on individualism that it is allowed to

stymie the procurement of goods that are attainable only through rights-violating means.[4]

After asserting "that basic rights rest on an individualist foundation," Lomasky remarks that "it is the language of rights, more than any other component of our moral lexicon, that accents the special value of individualism" (PRM 11). One who challenges this view is Larry May. May holds that individuals can be unified by common interests and common purposes and, on the basis of a shared identity (such as being Muslim or Jewish), suffer what he calls "group-based harm." Therefore, he says, social groups can have rights as well as responsibilities.[5] Nevertheless, he denies the reality of groups as such, reducing a group to "individuals in relationships."[6] In so doing, May obscures two distinctions: first, that between harm done to individual members of a community because they belong to it (as by those who refuse to rent or sell residences to them) and harm done to a group or community as such (for example, genocide, which aims to destroy the community as well as eliminate its members); second, that between a right of a community itself (such as a right of national sovereignty) and a right in which the members of a community share collectively (such as the right to communicate in their own language or dialect). He also obscures the difference between a community of people who are actually involved in relations with one another—for instance, the members of an organization—and a community of persons who may be only potentially related—such as the scattered community of all who understand Polish.

Besides holding only individuals to be rights-bearers, some writers hold that rights belong to individuals taken independently rather than in relation to one another. This atomistic view is usually associated with an egoistic conception of personal motivation. As Lewis P. Hinchman points out, this is the view of both Hobbes and Locke. Viewing all rights after the model of liberties, and taking these to involve merely the absence of any interference with personal action, thinkers of this school take rights to be "non-correlative," meaning that "they do not imply any duty on the part of others to secure those rights for us." Hinchman notes that this conception coexists, in both Hobbes and Locke, with a conception of society on the analogy of a brick wall: just as the identity of a brick is independent of its being part of a wall, so the identity of an individual member of society is taken by them to be independent of his social and political relations. "There is," for them, "nothing inherently social or political about man."[7] Similarly, it would seem that there is nothing inherently social or political about rights, which are attributed by these thinkers to individuals *qua* individuals. Voicing a contemporary version of the same view, H. L. A. Hart states, in a well-known essay, "Rights are typically conceived of as *possessed* or *owned by* or *belonging to* individuals . . . a kind of moral property of individuals to which they are as individuals entitled."[8] Despite his strongly individualist commitment, Lomasky objects to this view: "[F]rom a starting point of nakedly egoistic agents for whom all value whatsoever is personal," he charges, "there is no egress" (PRM 69). Instead, he argues that part of the basis for rights is that "[t]he constraints of multipersonal interaction provide reason for each person to insist on being accorded the same level of forbearance from others that he is willing to accord to each of them" (PRM 77). And he sees this willingness as rooted in the intrinsic sociality of human beings and their capacity for empathy with one another.

A PRIORISM

Individualism in the theory of rights, especially that of the egoistic or atomistic sort just discussed, is often linked to what I have called *a priorism*. Rights are taken to be *a priori* in two senses: first, their existence is sometimes held to be self-evident—a view called, by A. P. d'Entrèves, 'rationalism';[9] and, second, they are most often said to be antecedent to, not dependent upon, the membership of those who have them in any community or society.

Both types of a priorism are common among theories of so-called 'natural rights'. The idea of natural rights grew out of the Christian tradition of natural law; but Hugo Grotius gave natural law a secular formulation, holding it to be a body of rules that man is able to discover by the use of his reason.[10] This is the view on which both Hobbes and Locke based their different versions of natural rights. Nevertheless, the religious associations (Protestant as well as Catholic) remained, as we see in the phraseology of the American Declaration of Independence, which talks of a people's assuming "the separate and equal station to which the Laws of Nature and of Nature's God entitle them," and states, in the well-known phrases, that "We hold these truths to be self-evident, that all men are created equal, that they are endowed by their Creator with certain unalienable Rights, that among these are Life, Liberty and the pursuit of Happiness." (The last, of course, is a substitute for Locke's "property.")

For Robert Nozick, who makes *a priori* rights the ground for anarchism, the existence of inviolable individual rights is a primary assumption, accepted, along with the rest of Locke's "state-of-nature" theory, without question. Writing in 1974, he points out that:

> Individuals in Locke's state of nature are in 'a state of perfect freedom to order their actions and dispose of their possessions and persons as they think fit, within the bounds of the law of nature, without asking leave or dependency upon the will of any other man' (John Locke, *Two Treatises of Government*, sect. 4). The bounds of the law of nature require that 'no one ought to harm another in his life, health, liberty, or possessions' (sect. 6). Some persons transgress these bounds, 'invading others' rights and . . . doing hurt to one another,' and in response people may defend themselves or others against such invaders of rights (chap. 3). . . . [E]veryone has a right to punish the transgressors of that law to such a degree as may hinder its violation . . . (sect. 7).[11]

Nevertheless, this right to punish transgressors is not taken to be in any way as constitutive of other rights.

Nozick himself, a strenuous a priorist, assumes "a state of nature that begins with fundamental general descriptions of morally permissible and impermissible actions," implying that normative or prescriptive principles can be inherent in nature.[12] In a well-known and much respected essay, British philosopher Margaret MacDonald shows that this assumption, which is part of all natural rights theories, rests on a failure to distinguish three very different kinds of statement: tautologies, empirical or contingent propositions (statements of fact), and assertions of value. "Because it is confused on these distinctions, the theory of natural law and natural rights constantly confuses reason with right and both with

matter of fact and existence."[13] The rights taken to be "natural"
are not supposed to be established by any positive law or human
commitment. That all human beings have these rights (which, be
it remembered, are differently identified by different theorists) is
taken by them all to be a matter of fact, following tautologically
from the definition of human nature. But a tautological conclusion based on a definition is not a matter of fact. That such a law
exists cannot be entailed by any definition, and MacDonald denies
that there is "a law governing the relations of human beings as
such, independently of the laws of all particular societies . . ."
(NR 23).[14] The statement that there "is" such a law, she says, is
deceptive in its grammar: the natural law theorist is not making
"a statement of verifiable fact about the actual constitution of the
world," but stating that there *ought* to be such a law. Saying that
"there is" such a law states an ideal, which, rather than being a
fact, sets up a standard for human society. "Assertions about natural rights . . . are assertions of what ought to be as the result of
human choice. They [are] expressions of value," value judgments
(NR 34). But, MacDonald notes, these judgments are not simply
those of the individuals who make these statements. They express
fundamental values of the societies from which they emanate.
This is why they seem to be "natural." "[T]he fundamental values
of a society are not always recorded in explicit decisions by its
members, even its rulers, but are expressed in the life of the society and constitute its quality. . . . [They are made], explicitly or
by acceptance, by those who live and work in a society and operate its institutions." They are "decisions . . . not true or false and
. . . not deduced from premises" (NR 35–36, 37). There may be
considerations which support them. In the case of those values
we call rights, "[i]t is the emphasis on the individual sufferer from
bad social conditions which constitutes the appeal of the social
contract theory and the 'natural' origin of human rights" (NR
30). But even when the (actual or potential) practical effects of
the enforcement of rights justify them to us, this justification is
not conclusive. Not only are human rights not self-evident; but
as values, they cannot be asserted with either logical or empirical
certainty.

Assertions that "there are" rights are value judgments of a special sort; they are prescriptive or normative—"oughts." And if

this is the case, we cannot justify rights by arguing deductively. Hume has taught us that we cannot infer an 'ought' from an 'is'. Recognizing this, Gewirth speaks of the existence of rights as "normative existence." He utilizes this concept in an effort to bridge the "is–ought gap" and to show that we can logically justify the statement 'there is a right to x', after all. In a lengthy argument designed to show the logical necessity of the existence of what he calls the basic or "generic" human rights ("equivalent to 'natural' rights"), Gewirth maintains that because humans are agents, and freedom and well-being are necessary conditions of action—necessary goods—"no person can rationally disavow either the necessary goods or the consequent human rights [to those goods]" (HR 7). That is, the statement that because they are agents all humans have the rights to freedom and well-being is tautologous. Rawls offers a similar argument, holding that persons in a hypothetical "original position" of ignorance regarding their own social status would rationally have to choose his two principles of justice. The first of these is a principle of rights: the principle that "each person is to have an equal right to the most extensive system of equal basic liberties compatible with a similar system of liberty for all" (TJ 302). If each of us, unknown to ourselves, could be in any social position from the top to the bottom of the scale, it would be self-evident to us, he holds, that no position should be disadvantaged by carrying with it fewer rights than others.

Even if they do not find them to be self-evident, many writers take the basic human rights to be antecedent to membership in society. Hart, for instance, who argues for the equal right of all men to be free being a natural right, says, "This right is one which all men have . . . *qua* men and not only if they are members of some society or stand in some special relation to each other" (AT 15). In the words of Virginia Held, who is distinguishing moral from legal rights, "we can claim our moral rights even if a given society fails to recognize them or is unable or unwilling to assure them in practice."[15] And, defending natural rights, David A. Hoekema says "that all persons have certain rights simply as persons. . . . We all have certain natural or moral rights, in other words; these rights belong to all persons simply as persons and are not created by legal and social systems. Such rights are extrasocietal, not in the sense that they cannot be supported by the force of law or other social sanctions, but in the sense that they are rights which everyone has even in the absence of such support."[16]

Opposing this view, Martin Golding maintains that "every claim of right makes implicit reference to a community," for outside a social environment "rights-discourse has no foothold."[17] "The type of community that gives rise to talk of rights," he tells us, "is one in which there are at least two individuals who are capable of communicating demands, have a capacity to respond to demands, and whose demands may clash."[18] (Note that this view presupposes an adversarial conception of rights.) Golding's position is endorsed by W. T. Blackstone: "Rights talk . . . presupposes conflicts of interests. . . . The notion of persons who press claims against other persons clearly implies the notion of a human community, small or large."[19] On somewhat different grounds, and attacking both forms of a priorism, Richard Flathman states: "Contrary to the impression often given by natural rights theorists from Locke to Robert Nozick, rights are not natural, divine, primitive, or brute facts. Nor are they somehow self-justifying or self-evidently justified."[20] This is because rights "arise out of and are accorded within a rule-governed social practice" (PR 6). (Flathman takes rights themselves to be social practices.) Flathman's view, which he calls "civic individualism," hews a line between individualism and so-called "communitarianism," which sees individual rights as a threat to communally held values (PR 8–9).

> [T]here is a great gulf between the conception of the individual and individual rights advanced by natural rights theorists and the practice of rights as it operates in contemporary Western societies. . . . [R]ights as we know them would be impossible in the absence of a rather elaborate array of arrangements and structures. . . . What is more, it is in and through these arrangements and structures that individuals develop interests and purposes and acquire rights to act on them [PR 188].

His justification of rights expresses this dual emphasis on social arrangements and individual interests and purposes. Nevertheless, it is individual rights that he is justifying. Not an a priorist, he is still an individualist. To begin with, he invokes a *"liberal principle,* a normative principle according to which it is a prima facie good for individuals to have and be in a position to act upon and satisfy their interests and desires, objectives and purposes" (PR 7). Assuming this, he says that the justification for what he calls "the Great Rights," which are the political rights of speech, press, and association, habeas corpus, and the right to free and equal suffrage, "is that they serve important interests of the individuals who exercise them and also protect arrangements, institutions, and norms important to all members who value a sociopolitical order of the type in question," that is, the type of society in which these rights could be exercised (PR 220).

ESSENTIALISM

The principle I am calling 'essentialism' is intrinsic to natural rights theories and, in most formulations, also asserts the priority of rights to membership in a community. Essentialism is a doctrine (or a family of doctrines) concerning the basis or ground of rights and the prerequisites or criteria of eligibility for rights. It locates these either in human nature as such or in some characteristic or power taken to be an essential trait of human beings. As it is by Kant, humanity is elevated by some natural rights theorists to the status of an absolute value.[21] A classic statement of such a view, rooted in Christian natural law doctrine, is that of Jacques Maritain: "[N]atural law and the light of moral conscience within us do not prescribe merely things to be done and not to be done. They also recognize rights, in particular rights bound up with the very nature of man." Maritain distinguishes these fundamental human rights from civic rights and more narrowly social rights such as the rights of workers. "The human person," he says, "has rights by the very fact that he is a person, a whole who is master of himself and of his acts, and consequently not merely a means, but an end, an end which must be treated as such." Asserting the existence of fundamental human rights such as those of existence and life and the right to personal freedom, Maritain claims that "all these rights are rooted in the vocation of the person, a spiritual and free agent, to the order of absolute values and to a destiny superior to time."[22]

Margaret MacDonald rejects the contention underlying Maritain's claim: namely, that "there is a human nature and this human nature is the same in all men . . . and possessed of a nature, constituted in a given determinate fashion, man obviously possesses ends which correspond to his natural constitution and which are the same for all . . ." (NR 29).[23] Against this, she holds,

> Men do not share a fixed nature, nor, therefore, are there any ends which they must necessarily pursue in fulfilment of such nature. There is no definition of 'man'. There is a more or less vague set of properties which characterize in varying degrees and proportions those creatures which are called human. . . . There is no end set for the human race by an abstraction called 'human nature'. There are only ends which individuals choose, or are forced by circumstances to accept [NR 39–40].

Maritain's Catholic version of essentialism is cast in part in terms of the Kantian thesis that a human being is not merely a means but an end "which must be treated as such." Contemporary rights-theorists of a more naturalistic stripe seek a basis for treating human beings as rights-holders in their possession of selected human characteristics, with no general agreement as to what these are. In introducing his own theory of human rights, Gewirth says, "Human rights are a species of moral rights: they are moral rights which all persons equally have simply because they are human" (HR 1). In amplifying this statement, he identifies the human characteristic on which he rests his argument for rights as that of rational agency. Because all men are rational agents, he contends (as I have already noted) that they must, on pain of contradiction, hold that they have the rights to the necessary conditions of action, freedom, and well-being, in the absence of which no one could act.

Lomasky cites being a "project pursuer" and being capable of understanding the motivation of others, both of which he takes to be universal human characteristics, as jointly providing a moral argument for basic rights. "Project pursuers," he says,

> whatever their projects may be, value the ability to be a pursuer of projects. That means that they value having moral space. Because rights demarcate moral space, every project pursuer has reason to desire to be accorded the status of a rights holder. . . . Each project

pursuer, whatever his projects may be, is fully on a par with every other project pursuer in having reason to value the advancement of his own projects above the advancement of all others. And each is aware that every other project pursuer has exactly the same reason personally to value his own project pursuit in virtue of its being his [PRM 60, 78].

This awareness being mutual and reciprocal, all alike desire the existence of an enforcement mechanism to ensure that they are given the "moral space" in which to pursue their own projects. This enforcement mechanism is the establishment of the equal right of all. While this does not guarantee that rights will actually be established in any given community (or, Lomasky remarks, between communities), he takes it to provide a justification for the institution of rights that everyone should accept.

There is a modified or extended version of essentialism, which might be called 'proto-humanism', whose proponents hold whatever feature it is that they take to qualify humans for rights to be also shared by nonhumans who, thereby, are also endowed with rights. Contending that we do in fact ascribe rights to animals, Joel Feinberg holds the property in virtue of which we do so to be the capacity to have interests.[24] Not only does he find animals to have interests, he extends "the interest principle" so as "to permit us to ascribe rights to infants, fetuses, and generations yet unborn." Most proponents of fetal rights claim that human fetuses, or even fertilized human ova, are already human beings; they possess the essence of humanity. Appealing instead to the interest principle, Feinberg justifies his extension of it "on the grounds that interests can exert a claim upon us even before their possessors actually come into being."[25] That is, rights protect and are justified by *potential* as well as actual interests—or even (a point that Feinberg overlooks) by merely possible future interests. Tom Regan, the well-known champion of animal rights, holds that the basis of rights is "inherent value," the value, according to him, of "beings with beliefs, desires, the faculties of perception and memory, an emotional life, a sense of the future, preferences, the capacity for suffering."[26] Peter Singer maintains that only consciousness, not self-consciousness or the ability to have long-range purposes, characterizes all human beings without exception, including those who are severely mentally defective. He therefore concludes that only their being conscious (which includes the capacity for suffering) makes it wrong for us to kill human beings or make them suffer. He argues that because animals are similarly conscious, to attribute lesser worth or dignity to them than to humans and to relegate them to a lesser moral status is to be guilty of "speciesism," an arbitrary and unjustified preference for our own kind.[27] It follows that if we grant humans the right to life and the right to be spared the gratuitous infliction of pain, we ought to grant nonhuman animals the same rights. Against this, I have argued that participation in the social relations that constitute rights in practice requires specific capacities or powers, so that none of the criteria cited is by itself sufficient.

Adversarialism

Most contemporary rights theorists, even those who are concerned with what they call "moral" or "human" rights, have a legalistic or "forensic" view in terms of which to have a right is to have *a claim against* other persons or against society. Rawls, for instance, as noted above, takes rights to be principles for "ordering the conflicting claims of moral persons." As Rawls's phrase suggests, even though most of them take rights to be possessed by individuals, writers who have this view covertly introduce a relational conception of rights, portraying them as adversarial relations. The figure on whom many, if not most, of these thinkers rely for their definition of a right is the legal theorist Wesley N. Hohfeld, for whom the notion of a right in what he calls the strictest sense is that of a claim.[28] As explicated by Judith Jarvis Thomson, who follows Hohfeld, to say X has a right is to say,

> X has a claim against Y that p (where p states that Y is to perform a particular act).

She takes this to be equivalent to the statement that

> Y is under a duty toward X, namely the duty that Y discharges only if p.[29]

As Thomson goes on to say, "every claim is a right that an entity *has against an entity*" (RR 41). As Lomasky puts it, in using the language of rights, we are talking about "the justified claims of individuals against their governments and against each other" (PRM 11). (Adversarialism here is linked to individualism.) Alan Gewirth, too, sees "the full structure" of a right, i.e., what Hohfeld calls a 'claim' or 'claim-right', to have the form of an adversarial relation. In Gewirth's formulation,

A has a right to X against B by virtue of Y

where A and B are individual agents, X is some good that is the object of the right, and Y is a condition that justifies the claim (e.g., that B has made a promise or, in the case of the basic human rights, the argument or proof based on rational agency) (HR 2).[30] H. J. McCloskey tries to refute this analysis of rights as adversarial by appealing to what I have called an 'atomistic' conception. A right, he says, is "not a right against some vague group of potential or possible obstructors."[31] He uses as an example the right to life: "My right to life is not a right against anyone. It is my right and by virtue of it, it is normally permissible for me to sustain my life in the face of obstacles."[32] McCloskey does not deny that we can have some rights against others but these are derivative. My right to life, he says, "does give rise to rights against others *in the sense* that others have or may come to have duties to refrain from killing me, but it is essentially a right of mine, not an infinite list of claims, hypothetical and actual, against an infinite number of actual, potential, and as yet nonexistent human beings."[33] In a counter-argument, Feinberg insists that "[w]hether we are speaking of claims or rights . . . we must notice that they seem to have two dimensions, as indicated by the prepositions 'to' and 'against'. . . . All rights seem to merge *entitlements to* do, have, omit, or be something with *claims against* others to act or refrain from acting in certain ways."[34]

Flathman, whom I mentioned earlier as trying to avoid a strict individualist position, seems to take a divergent view regarding adversarialism as well, contending that when A has a right, the relationship between A and B is one of "reciprocity." "It is ordinarily the case," he points out, "that an agent who is an *A* with right X in context 1 may be a *B* with regard to the same X in context 2," and "[t]he same is true of *B*." And, he continues, "participants in the practice readily and regularly switch from one role to the other in the course of interactions in the practice" (PR 86–87). As I shall show, this is closer to my own view. Nevertheless, the rights he is talking about are still portrayed adversarially (as well as individualistically): "If Jones has a right against Smith, Jones can oblige Smith to act in a manner contrary to Smith's interests [and vice versa]" (PR 87). In fact (having liberties in mind), Flathman defines rights in the general sense "as protections against interferences from all other parties," a special case of this being "protection of individual freedom of action against interference by the state" (PR 159). Furthermore, it is of the essence of a right, as he sees it, that it justifies obligating others to act contrary to their own interests. Thus, the reciprocity in question pits the interests of individual rights-bearers against those of one another.

Not all who adopt this adversarial view of rights are individualist in the sense of denying rights to communities. Speaking with particular reference to the provision, in the United Nations Covenants on Civil and Political Rights and on Economic, Social and Cultural Rights, conferring rights upon "peoples," and also to the Genocide Convention of 1948, Gillian Triggs recognizes both the rights of peoples and those of states. She cautions, furthermore, that "if peoples' rights are to have any meaning beyond States' rights, they must include the right of a 'people' against its own government."[35]

In contrast to this pervasive adversarial view, and also in contrast to both a priorism and atomism, George Herbert Mead, a contemporary and associate of John Dewey's, suggests that a right is a mutual relation that has evolved among the members of a community. According to Mead, "the individual in asserting his own right is also asserting that of all other members of the community."[36] He finds the source of this notion in Jean-Jacques Rousseau's version of the contractarian theory of society. As over against Thomas Hobbes, Rousseau holds that the people can be sovereign in themselves, and they are so "in so far as they exercise a *volonté générale*." Mead takes this to mean that not only can the people as a whole exercise sovereignty, but also that each of them as an individual, every member of a community, "can be both subject and sovereign," and is so "if his will is the will of the community. . . . [A] man as an individual in the community can act not simply as a representative of himself or for himself but for the whole community if his will is identical with the will of the other members of the community."[37] This principle is the source of the authority that the law has in a rational state. "If laws express the will of the community," Mead says, "the individual is able both to enact them and to obey them as a member of the community" (MT 13). All members of the community being equally authors and subjects of the law and, as authors, expressing the same general will, on the one hand, each is legislating to all and all to each; on the other hand, as members of the community for which they are legislating, each is thereby commanding himself to obey the will of all and all to obey the will of each.

In his own theory of society, Mead broadens Rousseau's concept of the general will and its authority, asserting the existence of what he calls "the attitude of the generalized other," the attitude of the whole community (MSS 154). Rather than being the community's will, the attitude of the generalized other encompasses all the understandings that are shared by its members and that govern both their lives together and their relations to one another. That is, it consists in what sociologists call the social norms: the principles and concepts that all members of the community are expected to internalize and that provide the parameters in terms of which they govern their own behavior and interpret that of one another.[38] The norms operative in any community define the behaviors and verbal expressions that are appropriate in those social situations and contexts which feature in the life of that community, and also the responses these behaviors and expressions call for. For Mead, as a Pragmatist, the response that any action or expression is understood to call for constitutes its meaning. In prescribing the responses that may be given to gestures or utterances, the norms that constitute the attitude of a generalized other enable the members of that community to understand one another: they enable them to interact communicatively and purposively as well as to communicate in the narrower sense of this term. This attitude is "general," or "generalized," in the sense that it is not the point of view of any one member of the community or of someone playing any particular role. Instead, it is an inclusive perspective, encompassing the attitudes and understandings proper to all the roles involved in the life of that community—the norms governing all the roles and the mutually responsive behaviors they involve.[39] Anyone who has internalized the general attitude of the community will have, as part of his or her perspective as a self, a set of attitudes that makes it possible to take not only the point of view proper to that person's own position or role, but also that of any other role in that community. This enables any of us to put ourselves in the place of any of the others, to "see ourselves as others see us"—i.e., to understand our own behavior as others do. In this way we can know what they expect of us, which is what we would expect of them were they in our position.

Mead explains this by means of an analogy: a special case of the attitude of a generalized other, namely, the rules of a game. Having learned the rules of, say, baseball or soccer, one knows what is involved in playing any position on any team. Having internalized the rules, any potential or actual player has the general attitude or perspective common to all—the attitude of the community of players. He therefore knows which actions are permissible and which are not, and knows how any given action, including his own, may be interpreted; what the legitimate responses to it are. Rules are one kind of social norm. As rules govern a game, the social norms govern (or, as Mead sometimes says, they are) the institutions of a community, the institution of rights among them. As Margaret MacDonald would put it, social norms are the judgments of communities, evolving in the history of their members' joint efforts to coordinate their behavior and communicate with one another. In participating—as we all do—in the development and perpetuation of a set of norms, an individual participates in shaping the comprehensive attitude of a generalized other. Norms governing the institution of rights are constituents of this attitude. This is to say that it is a community, in generating the attitude of the generalized other, that institutes rights and confers the entitlements and the duties that those rights entail.

To claim that one has a right is to play a role defined by the attitude of the generalized other—the community—and to say, implicitly, that one is acting as a representative member of that community, any of whom may play the same role. If this were not the case, what one is taking to be a right would not be such: this is part of what the assertion of a right means. It is what distinguishes a claim of right from any other claim. To perform an action that is called for in response to the assertion of a right *because* one understands that response to be the one that is called for is also to act as a representative member of the community and to play the role defined by the attitude of the generalized other as the proper response to the rights-claim. To respect a right as being such, no less than to assert one's own or another's right, is to say, implicitly, that everyone else, including the one who is asserting the right, is also expected to respect it and, when called upon, to behave accordingly. Again, this is part of what it means for a right to exist—part of the institution of rights. As Mead said, again building on Rousseau, "rights exist only in so far as they are acknowledged, and only to the extent that those who claim them acknowledge them in the person of others. That is, no man can claim a right which he does not recognize for others. No man can claim a right who does not at the same time affirm his own obligation to respect that right in all others" (MT 13).[40]

And, again talking about Rousseau's doctrine but expressing his own view as well, Mead confers a special importance upon rights as binding us together in community rather than setting us against one another or against society: "If men are capable of recognizing rights as well as of claiming them, then they are capable of forming a community, of establishing institutions whose authority will lie within the community itself" (MT 13).

NOTES

1. Alan Gewirth, *Human Rights: Essays on Justification and Applications* (Chicago: The University of Chicago Press, 1982), p. 12; hereafter cited as HR.

2. Lon Fuller, *Legal Fictions* (Stanford, California: Stanford University Press, 1967).

3. John Rawls, *A Theory of Justice* (Cambridge, Massachusetts: The Belknap Press of Harvard University Press, 1971), pp. 133–134, 521 (emphasis added); hereafter cited as TJ.

4. Loren Lomasky, *Persons, Rights, and the Moral Community* (New York: Oxford University Press, 1987), pp. 16–17; hereafter cited as PRM.

5. Larry May, *The Morality of Groups* (Notre Dame, Indiana: Notre Dame University Press, 1989), e.g., pp. 38, 73ff., 112ff.

6. Ibid., p. 9.

7. Lewis P. Hinchman, "The Origins of Human Rights: A Hegelian Perspective," *Western Political Quarterly*, 37, No. 1 (March 1984), 11–12.

8. H. L. A. Hart, "Are There Any Natural Rights?" *The Philosophical Review*, 64 (April 1955); repr. in *Rights*, ed. David Lyons (Belmont, California: Wadsworth Publishing Co., 1979), p. 19; hereafter cited as AT.

9. A. P. d'Entrèves, *Natural Law: An Historical Survey* (London: Hutchinson University Library, 1951; repr. New York: Harper Torchbooks, 1965), p. 49.

10. Hugo Grotius, *Laws of War and Peace* (1625), trans. F. W. Kelsey, The Classics of International Law 3 (Washington, D.C.: Carnegie Endowment for International Peace, 1925); cf. d'Entrèves, *Natural Law*, pp. 50–52.

11. Robert Nozick, *Anarchy, State, and Utopia* (New York: Basic Books, 1974), p. 10. Nozick's references to Locke's *Two Treatises of Government* of 1690 are to Peter Laslett's edition (Cambridge: Cambridge University Press, 1963).

12. Nozick, *Anarchy, State, and Utopia*, p. 7.

13. Margaret MacDonald, "Natural Rights," *Proceedings of the Aristotelian Society* (1947–48); repr. in *Theories of Rights*, ed. Jeremy Waldron (Oxford: Oxford University Press, 1989), p. 26; hereafter cited as NR.

14. The belief that the conclusion that all humans have rights is tautological assumes what I shall call 'essentialism,' namely, that "[there] must . . . be an essential human nature which determines this status [i.e., that of rights-bearer]" (NR 23–24). As we shall see, MacDonald denies this as well.

15. Virginia Held, *Rights and Goods: Justifying Social Action* (New York: The Free Press, 1984), p. 15.

16. David A. Hoekema, *Rights and Wrongs: Coercion, Punishment, and the State* (Selinsgrove, Pennsylvania: Susquehanna University Press; London and Toronto: Associated University Presses, 1986), p. 89.

17. Martin P. Golding, "Towards a Theory of Human Rights," *The Monist*, 52, No. 4 (October 1968), 528.

18. Ibid.

19. W. T. Blackstone, "Equality and Human Rights," *The Monist*, 52, No. 4 (October 1968), 629.

20. Richard E. Flathman, *The Practice of Rights* (Cambridge: Cambridge University Press, 1976), p. 2; hereafter cited as PR.

21. Cf. John T. Noonan, Jr., "An Almost Absolute Value in History," in *The Morality of Abortion: Legal and Historical Perspectives*, ed. John T. Noonan, Jr. (Cambridge, Massachusetts: Harvard University Press, 1970); excerpt in *Philosophical Issues in Human Rights*, ed. Patricia H. Werhane, A. R. Gini, and David T. Ozar (New York: Random House, 1986).

22. Jacques Maritain, *The Rights of Man and Natural Law*, trans. Doris C. Anson (New York: Harcourt, Brace, 1943), Chapter 4, "Human Rights."

23. On Maritain, see NR, p. 35.

24. Joel Feinberg, "The Rights of Animals and Unborn Generations," in *Philosophy and Environmental Crisis*, ed. William Blackstone (Athens: University of Georgia Press. 1974); repr. in *Philosophical Issues in Human Rights*, ed. Patricia H. Werhane, A. R. Gini, and David T. Ozar (New York: Random House, 1986), pp. 164–173.

25. Ibid., pp. 169–170.

26. Tom Regan, *All That Dwell Therein* (Berkeley and Los Angeles: University of California Press, 1982); *The Case for Animal Rights* (Berkeley and Los Angeles: University of California Press, 1983).

27. Peter Singer, "Animals and the Value of Life," in *Matters of Life and Death: New Introductory Essays in Moral Philosophy*, ed. Tom Regan, 2nd ed. (New York: Random House, 1986); see also Singer's *Animal Liberation* (New York: Avon Books, 1977).

28. Wesley Newcomb Hohfeld, *Fundamental Legal Conceptions*, ed. W. W. Cook (New Haven, Connecticut: Yale University Press, 1919). This volume contains Hohfeld's seminal papers from the *Yale Law Journal* of 1913 and 1917 under the title "Some Fundamental Legal Conceptions as Applied in Judicial Reasoning."

29. Judith Jarvis Thomson, *The Realm of Rights* (Cambridge, Massachusetts: Harvard University Press, 1990), p. 41; hereafter cited as RR.

30. Gewirth distinguishes, as Hohfeld does, between claims or claim-rights and liberties, powers, or immunities, but assumes that "human rights are entirely or mainly kinds of claim-rights" and treats this as the model of a right.

31. H. J. McCloskey, "Rights," *Philosophical Quarterly*, 15 (1965), 118.

32. Ibid.

33. Ibid.

34. Joel Feinberg, "The Nature and Value of Rights," in *Rights*, ed. David Lyons (Belmont, California: Wadsworth Publishing Co., 1979), p. 91.

35. Gillian Triggs, "The Rights of Peoples and Individual Rights:

Conflict or Harmony?" in *The Rights of Peoples*, ed. James Crawford (Oxford: Clarendon Press, 1988), p. 142.

36. George Herbert Mead, "Natural Rights and the Theory of the Political Institution," *The Journal of Philosophy, Psychology, and Scientific Methods*, 12 (1915), 141–155; repr. in *George Herbert Mead: Selected Writings*, ed. Andrew J. Reck (Indianapolis: Bobbs-Merrill, 1964), p. 163; hereafter cited as PI. See also Mead's *Mind, Self, and Society: From the Standpoint of a Social Behaviorist*, ed. Charles W. Morris (Chicago: The University of Chicago Press, 1934), pp. 164, 261, and passim; hereafter cited as MSS.

37. George Herbert Mead, *Movements of Thought in the Nineteenth Century*, ed. Merritt H. Moore (Chicago: The University of Chicago Press, 1936), pp.16–17; hereafter cited as MT.

38. "Norms" is not Mead's word, but it is the contemporary term that best conveys what Mead intends when he talks of the attitude of a generalized other.

39. Mead speaks of these behaviors as "gestures," and he speaks of mutually responsive gestures, those whose respective meanings—the responses they call for—are governed by the attitude of a generalized other, as "significant symbols."

40. In being something of which all the members of the community in which the institution of rights exists have a common understanding, a right is what Mead calls "a common social object" (PI 163). Cf. T. H. Green: "[R]ights . . . are constituted by . . . mutual recognition. . . . It is only a man's consciousness of having an object in common with others, a well-being which is consciously his in being theirs and theirs in being his—only the fact that they are recognised by him and he by them as having this object—that gives him the claim described" (*Lectures on the Principles of Political Obligation*, ed. Paul Harris and John Morrow [Cambridge: Cambridge University Press, 1968], p. 144).

2

An Alternative to the Dominant Tradition

I

What Is a Right?

WHAT, EXACTLY, IS A RIGHT? Surprisingly, there is no definition
on which all rights theorists will agree, and many simply take the
concept for granted. Most contemporary writers in the field define rights as claims; some see them not simply as claims, but as
claims to which there are reciprocal duties or obligations. Wesley
Hohfeld asks, regarding the term 'right', "what clue do we find
. . . toward limiting the word in question to a definite and appropriate meaning?" His answer is, "That clue lies in the correlative
'duty'."[1] In Thomson's version, "X's having a claim [against Y]
is equivalent to Y's being under a duty."[2] This does not mean
that every duty is a duty to satisfy a rights–claim. Supposing that
there is a moral duty to be charitable, no one has a right to charity.
Nevertheless, as Alan Gewirth puts it, "There is a logical correla-
tivity between 'A has a right to X' on the one hand, and, on the
other, 'Other persons ought to [i.e., have a duty to] refrain from
interfering with A's having X and ought, also, under certain circumstances, to assist A to have X'.[3]

Whether or not they agree that there is a duty correlative to
every right, many others also speak of rights as claims. But there
are some problems with this usage. For instance, despite Hohfeld's
use of 'claim' as a synonym for 'right' in what he calls the strictest
sense, he distinguishes between claim-rights and the kinds of
rights he calls powers and liberties; and there are others who conceive rights as essentially liberties.

Moreover, there is an ambiguity in the way the word 'claim' is
used: we can be said to have a claim and also to make or assert a

claim, with the somewhat confusing consequence that we can claim something to which we have no claim. Thus, some hold that a right is a justified or, as Feinberg prefers to say, a valid claim.[4] I prefer a different solution, which avoids both sorts of problem.

One who "has a right," in the conventional sense of this expression, is entitled to possess something, to act in a particular way, or to be accorded a particular sort of treatment. That is, she or he has an entitlement. Virginia Held contends that "[m]oral rights are stringent entitlements yielded by valid moral principles."[5] But if rights are entitlements, what is the relation between rights and duties? Should we define a right as an entitlement to which there is a correlative duty? Is this duty in some sense constitutive of the right? Or is it only implied by an entitlement that has been established as a right independently?

Not every entitlement counts as a right. One may be entitled to praise for doing something well, but nobody would call this entitlement a right. For it to be a right, the praise would have to be obligatory, owed. It would be a duty. But duties are specific actions; for example, Thomson's illustration of her definition of a right: "A has a claim against B that B stay off A's land." But there can be more than one action whose performance is required by a given rights-entitlement (if A has a right to his land—is entitled to its possession and use—B may also have a duty not to erect any structure that will block A's access to his land). And circumstances could arise in which additional actions, as yet unanticipated, would be called for. In addition, there are entitlements that can be fulfilled in alternative ways. (If there is a right to health care, it can be satisfied by providing a national health system like Canada's, or by making private health care or private health insurance affordable, or by passing a law requiring all employers to provide health insurance for their employees and their families—plus making some provision for care of the unemployed and their families.) In some cases, precisely which actions it is a duty to perform in order to satisfy a given entitlement is a matter of dispute. This is an important dimension of the struggle over "affirmative action" in the United States today. It is coming to be accepted that women and members of ethnic minorities have a right to be treated fairly. Some people (including writers and lawyers who

have testified before the United States Supreme Court) say that
people in both categories, who have higher rates of unemploy-
ment, seldom occupy high-level positions in business, industry, or
government, and receive proportionately fewer secondary-school
diplomas or college or university degrees, are thus disadvantaged
because they have been unfairly discriminated against historically
and, in some cases, continue to be discriminated against. (For instance, at least in our large cities, black children on average attend
schools that are more crowded, older, less well kept, and more
poorly equipped than do white children.) Therefore, some contend, it is only fair to give those who fall into these categories
preference in such things as hiring and college, graduate, and pro-
fessional school admissions, at least in cases where they are as well
qualified as other, nonminority candidates. (Some would say that
different criteria should be applied to them.) Others, however, insist that this so-called "affirmative action," as preferential treatment,
constitutes "reverse discrimination," and is inherently unfair.[6] If we
do take fair treatment to be a right, what, in such cases, is the duty
correlative to this right? If we have no generally accepted way of
satisfying this entitlement, should we, on the grounds that there is
no correlative duty, deny that it is or can be a right?

I suggest that we need to put the issue in a somewhat different
perspective. In any society in which the institution of rights is
operative, there is a general obligation to acknowledge rights and
to respect them whether or not we are called upon to express
this attitude in overt behavior. And when we are called upon to
implement a right, to satisfy an entitlement that counts as a right,
whatever action we choose to perform, this attitude should govern our performance. We ought to act out of respect for the
rights-entitlement in question, or, as Kant might put it, for the
sake of respecting it, and not for any other reason. It is this, rather
than the act per se (or, in some cases, rather than any particular
act), that is called for by the exercise of the right. Thus, instead of
saying that there are duties correlative to rights-entitlements, I
prefer to say that there is a correlative obligation to respect them,
binding upon all.[7] It is this obligation that distinguishes an entitlement that is a right from other entitlements. Apart from the obligation of all to respect it, which entails implementing this respect
in action when one is in a position to do so, the entitlement

would not be a right. Therefore, the norms making respect for it obligatory are constitutive of the right. To put it another way: the rights-entitlement and the obligation to respect it are constitutive of each other. This obligation is, of course, a duty; but stating it in the language I propose avoids the connotation of specificity that has come to be attached to the latter word, at least as it is employed in the literature of rights-theory.

A right, then, involves both an entitlement and a correlative obligation to respect it, and we could define a right as consisting of the two in their mutual relation. Strictly, a right *is* a relation—an institutionalized relation—between an entitlement and an obligation. To be accurate, we should speak of what we now call 'rights' as 'rights-entitlements'. However, the conventional usage, in which rights-entitlements are called 'rights', is almost unavoidable, and I shall use whichever term is clear in any particular context. But the conjunction of entitlement and obligation in an institutionalized rights-relation is not the whole story.

As both Gewirth and Margaret MacDonald remind us, the words 'entitlement' and 'obligation' (and the name 'right' as well) are not simply descriptive terms.[8] To say "X is entitled" or "X is obligated" is not to make a bare statement of fact; each of these statements has a prescriptive dimension. 'X is entitled' means that she *ought* to be permitted to do or to have whatever she is entitled to; 'X is obligated' means that he *ought* somehow to fulfill the obligation, to act so as to implement it or behave in such a way as to show that he acknowledges it. These meanings are established by the social norms. But they are not merely descriptive. They are prescriptive, directing us to behave in certain ways. The norms determining the entitlements and obligations associated with the institution and language of rights are rules of conduct, evolved by the community to govern certain of the relations among its members and carrying the community's authority. This authority is the source of their normative force. All who have internalized these normative principles are aware of their prescriptive character. They understand or feel (or are aware that they ought to do so) that they and everyone else should govern themselves by them and that it would be wrong not to. The language of rights expresses this understanding.

Insofar as they are internalized, therefore, and operative in governing the behavior and expectations of the members of the community, it is the social norms governing the institution of rights that effectively define and put into operation the entitlements and the obligations of those who participate in rights-relations. These norms are part of the attitude of the generalized other, the attitude of a community in which there are rights that are actually operative. Thus, the full definition of a right must include another term. It is not only a relation between an entitlement and an obligation to respect it. It is also a relation that exists in virtue of—hence, in relation to—the attitude of a generalized other. The rights-relation is a triadic one. Viewed in one way, the terms of this relation are the normative attitude, the entitlement, and the obligation it jointly establishes. It may also be seen as a relation between a community whose attitude encompasses rights–norms and any pair of its members, one in the position of entitlement, the other in that of being obligated to respect it. However, in principle every member of the community occupies both positions or roles: that of having the defined entitlement and that of being obligated to respect it, either role to be enacted as circumstances warrant. This is to say that the rights-relation is a mutual relation between each member of a community in which rights-norms are operative and each of the others, a relation that obtains in virtue of their sharing the attitude of a generalized other.

II

As a consequence of this analysis of rights, I reject all four of the interrelated principles or assumptions discussed in Chapter 1. I would like to explain why in some detail and show some of the ramifications and implications of my view. In the interest of clarity, I shall focus on each principle separately, but due to their interrelations, the treatment of each will involve discussion of others. I shall deal with them in the following order: the principle of a priorism, i.e., the assumption that rights are either self-evident or independent of social communities; the principle of adversarialism, i.e., the assumption that they are claims against other persons or against society or the State; the principle of essentialism, i.e., the assumption that the ground for the possession of rights lies in some essential trait of human (or quasi-human) nature as such; and the principle of individualism, i.e., the assumption that rights are inherently and exclusively properties of individuals.

A Priorism and the Concept of Universal Rights

Plainly, being conferred by a community through the establishment of norms, rights are not *a priori*. This has an important consequence. Linked to the assumption that rights are antecedent to membership in any community and also to the attribution of rights in virtue of human nature or personhood is the assertion, common to all natural rights theories, of the existence of universal human rights. But, on the proposed analysis, for a right to be operative, i.e., for it to exist, it must be institutionalized in a community, however wide or narrow that community may be; thus, the thesis that human rights are antecedent to society or that their existence is not dependent on rights-bearers' belonging to any community is falsified by definition. If any set of norms were universally operative among all humans, all humans would, in this respect even if not in others, constitute a single, universal normative community. If these norms were rights-norms, or included rights-norms among them, the rights these norms establish would be, *ipso facto*, universal human rights. Every human would participate in them, both as having the institutionalized entitlements and as being obligated to respect them, regardless of any other community affiliations. But they would still be operative in a community. And, clearly, some rights, such as the right to vote, which are linked to cultural institutions, are community based.

Mead at times suggests not only that there are universal rights, but also that to say that there is any particular right is to say that it is universal: "[R]ights exist," he says, "only in so far as they are acknowledged, and only to the extent that those who claim them acknowledge them in the person of others. That is, no man can claim a right which he does not recognize for others" (MT 13). On my proposed analysis, which derives in part from Mead, this is necessarily the case. Mead goes on to say, "No man can claim a right who does not at the same time affirm his own obligation to respect that right *in all others*" (MT 13; emphasis added). This implies that for anyone to claim or attribute a right is to affirm its universality, its universal existence. In practice, however, this cannot be the case, since a right will be operative—it will exist—only among those who do, in fact, share in the general attitude expressed by Mead's statement. In saying that there is a right, those who have the attitude governing it may mean to extend it to all others, and we would expect them to treat all others as if they were participants in the social institution of rights. But whatever rights we consider, there may be (and almost certainly are) communities in which those rights are neither recognized nor respected. This is to say that, while we may judge that certain rights ought to be universal, and even though those of us who have internalized rights-norms may act as though the rights we respect are universal, these and all other rights are fully operative only among those who have internalized the normative attitude of a community in which such rights are institutionalized. However, all who respect a given right and who claim it for themselves and attribute it to others constitute such a community, a community of the kind I call a 'normative community,' which is constituted by all who share a common set of norms. Regardless of geography, all who respect a given right belong to such a community. Moreover, all who respect rights of any kind, whichever rights those may be, constitute an extended community in which rights in general are recognized and respected. Furthermore, the perspective that they share (the attitude of a generalized other) enables them to discuss rights and deliberate as to which rights ought—or perhaps ought not—to be operative, either in their own communities or, universally, in all communities.

There is, as yet, no universal human community, even if we believe there ought to be. Even though the United Nations Declarations prescribe rights for all humans and all peoples, these rights are not universally operative—at least not yet. The claim to have a right that is not operative in a social community to which one belongs (for example, for a woman to claim equal rights with men in a patriarchal society) can mean only that the one who is making the claim believes that she and all others *ought* to have that right. Part of my theory of operative rights is an argument for universal rights (in my own terminology, 'generic rights'). However, I define these not in terms of a universal normative

community, the possibility of which I doubt, but as rights (entitlements with a correlative obligation to respect them) that ought to
be operative in every normative community. The specification of
'normative community' has a particular significance.

Very briefly summarized, my argument is this: The existence of
social norms, hence, of normative communities, is a prerequisite
of human life as we know it. All intelligible communication, all
meaningful social behavior, all coordinated social interaction is
norm-governed. Being the product of communicative interactions among the members of a community, social norms can be
established and perpetuated only by being accepted and applied
in the community. In addition, in order to apply the norms, one
must determine, first, whether they are really applicable to the
situation at hand and, if so, in what way or ways and, second,
how they should be applied. It is in this process that norms evolve
and change. For norms to arise in the first place, then, and for
them to carry the authority of a community, requires the participation of that community's members in their institution: it requires that they exercise their own personal authority in this
process. Therefore, freedom to exercise this authority in the life
of the community, the sphere in which the norms evolve and are
reinforced or modified, is a necessary condition of the evolution
and continuing existence of a normative community. Normative
community being a necessary condition of human existence, a
right of personal authority ought to be established in every community. But for norms to continue to be operative, they must be
recurrently applied and, if their application is not to be an invol-
untary performance (in which case the norms are likely to be
rejected) or an empty exercise (in which case they will lapse into
desuetude and lose their authority), those persons who are called
on or are in a position to apply them must be allowed to do so in
accordance with their own judgment and in the light of their own
experience. That is, they must be allowed to judge the norms
autonomously. Therefore, in addition to the right of personal authority, a right of personal autonomy should be made operative
in the ongoing life of every normative community. I call these the
fundamental generic rights: fundamental in that they are necessary
conditions for the continuing existence and stability of any nor-

mative community, and generic in the sense that they ought to be made universally operative.

Rights are often taken to be absolute, as well as universal, especially by those who view them as *a priori* and unconditioned by the social process to which they are supposed to apply. But the prescriptive force—the authority and presumed applicability—of rights-norms cannot be absolute or unquestionable. In the first place, more than one right may be applicable in a given situation, and these may conflict, so that the exercise of rights by one party may have to be at the expense of those of another. In an issue that was brought before the courts in the United States, so-called "hate speech" was held to be protected by the right of freedom of expression enshrined in the Bill of Rights. Against this, it was argued that such utterances infringe the right of those toward whom they are directed to be free of harassment. Plainly, these rights cannot prevail together, and a judgment is called for as to which should take precedence.

Rights may also come into conflict with other values. Especially by those who take them to exist *a priori*, rights are taken to be "trumps," which outweigh all contending principles in regulating social life. But other normative values may be judged in some situations to outweigh any given right. Even in communities where personal liberty is respected as a basic rights-entitlement, we do not hesitate to limit the liberty of a convicted criminal. More important, like all other forms of norm-governed social behavior, rights are *living* institutions. In any situation in which they come into play, not only may we sometimes find other norms to be applicable; we can also develop new understandings of what is at stake, new interpretations of or new insights into features of the situation or of the norms themselves or their consequences. We take these interpretations and insights into account in our personal deliberations and sometimes we introduce them into the social dialogue. This is to say that the operation of social norms does not preclude criticism (and, I contend, there can and ought to be a right or even an obligation of criticism). In actual fact, critical deliberation is part of the process in which norms are instituted, perpetuated, and modified. One place this process is systematically carried on is in the law courts. But not all social norms are ever enacted into law (think of the norms governing grammar and usage or those of dress), and there can be laws that never acquire the authority of the community at large so that they never become operative as social norms. Others lose that authority, so that even though they were once operative, they cease to be so. In the United States, for instance, the laws and norms governing minority rights have yet to keep pace with one another. Many people who would grant minorities equal treatment and who do so in their private lives or their own local communities have fought for legislation guaranteeing racial, sexual, and ethnic equality; yet there are laws establishing minority rights, such as the laws guaranteeing equal education and those prohibiting discrimination in the sale and rental of housing, that are openly flouted.

Adversarialism

One of the lessons we learn from Mead is that social norms, being attitudes of a "generalized other," enable those among whom they are operative to view the acts, things, and situations to which they are applicable in the same general perspective, allowing each of them to understand the responses of others even if these others have different social positions and roles. It is because we share the attitude of a generalized other that each of us understands his or her place and role in the complex social order in which we are located. Only by sharing a common understanding of the diverse roles in their mutual interrelatedness can we know how to play our own. The special feature of rights–norms is that, by their content, they confer upon all who are governed by them the reciprocal roles they establish, that of having rights (or rights-entitlements), and that of being obligated to respect those rights. In so doing, they establish a basis for mutual identification. Since for me to understand that I have a right is to understand you to have it as well, and vice versa, I also understand that if any of us can be arbitrarily deprived of this right, it is not really a right. I can see, therefore, that it is in my interest to protect your rights and I can show you that it is in your interest to protect mine. This mutuality that is inherent in rights-relations as I see them (and here, of course, I follow Mead) is directly contrary to the adversarial character attributed to them by those who conceive rights as claims against others. Not that one cannot bring suit against others to compel them to supply that to which one is entitled by right. But the unforced implementation of the rights-norms that are operative in everyday life is both a cause and a sign of social cohesion. A community in which those rights I have identified as fundamental and generic are operative, which I call a 'community of dialogic reciprocity', is one in which, regardless of their differences, each member recognizes and accepts as rights the autonomy and authority of all.[9] In such a community, could it exist, each member would understand that to respect the autonomy and authority of others is to protect one's own. Did such a community exist, it would embody the democratic ideal of unity in diversity: an ideal of the acceptance of difference, whether of opinion or of identity, together with a sharing of responsibility for decision-making and a willingness on the part of all to take one another's points of view seriously.

As we have seen, rights are also thought of as claims against society, against the community. The view proposed here is that as institutionalized social relations rights can exist only within communities and by the authority of those communities (that is, by the joint authority of their members). Operative rights are mutual relations among the members of those communities, not between a member and the community itself. Even a right such as the right to vote is an entitlement that all the members of the community are mutually obligated to respect and to implement as well as one in which they share. If and when a governmental body enforces the implementation of this or any right, it is acting in the name and by the authority of its members, who share the obligation to see that it is implemented. For a community to have rights *qua* community is, as I shall show, for it to participate as a member of a wider community in rights-relations that are similarly those of mutual entitlement and mutual obligation.

Before ending this section, I should like to point out that the rights-relation is a reflexive as well as an interpersonal one. Since each role is defined in terms of the other, nobody can have the attitude proper to one without at the same time having the attitude proper to the other. To claim a rights-entitlement, or even to recognize that one has it, is at the same time to express not only respect for that entitlement but recognition of the obligatory character of this respect. This is as true in relation to one's own claims as it is in relation to those of others.

Essentialism

Surprising as it may sound, as social institutions, rights are really traits of the communities in which they are operative, not of persons. In the strict sense of this term, it is not rights as such that members of a community have when rights are institutionalized there, but rights-entitlements and rights-obligations. Since these are operative only in the life of a community, it would seem that we have to seek the ground of rights in the nature of community or in the requirements of social interaction rather than in individual human nature or some feature thereof. Mead sees the mutual recognition of rights to be the expression of the attitude of a generalized other and, hence, to be a form of community. Agreeing with him, I agree as well that this attitude is generated in the effort to guide and direct the social process as such and the contributions of individuals to it. Thus, it seems to me that the institution of rights is grounded in, and rights are justified by, the requirements of social interaction. All social norms evolve out of the need of individuals to organize and coordinate their behavior, which requires them to know what to expect of others and what others expect of them as well as to have common purposes and goals and a shared understanding of these. In this process, among the norms that evolve are standards and values. Rights-norms, which themselves express value judgments, would seem to arise as ways of regulating the mutual relations of individuals in pursuit of their own goals and their other values—in pursuit, that is, of those things, statuses, liberties, powers, and so on, that have come to be judged valuable by the community and by those individuals themselves.

This does not mean, however, that there are no criteria for participation in rights. Participation presupposes the ability to internalize and govern oneself by social norms, and, in particular, to govern oneself by rights-norms: not only to respect rights-entitlements but to recognize and accept the obligation to do so, as well as to acknowledge others as having the same entitlements and to hold them, too, obligated to respect them. The ability to internalize and govern oneself by its norms is a necessary condition of membership in any normative community; the rest are specific to participation in the institution of rights. So neither human nature itself, nor any of the human characteristics taken by more conventional theorists to be the ground of rights—personhood, rationality, moral rationality, the power of agency, being a moral agent or a moral subject, being a project-pursuer, having interests—is specific enough to be the relevant criterion. The capacity for agency or rational or moral agency—the pursuit of projects—may be necessary conditions of rights behavior, but they are too general to be sufficient conditions, as is "humanity" (even if there is a universal human nature rather than indefinitely many characteristics that are typical of human beings but not necessarily shared by all). The contention that human beings and other animals have inherent value, and that this is the ground of rights, which is what Peter Singer asserts, is vulnerable on two counts. In the first place, as I have already pointed out, value is a judgment. As John Dewey would say, a value is a valuation, not a natural property. It is not inherent in any being. And even if it were, having inherent value would not confer upon the being possessed of it the powers that would enable it to participate in rights.

In the second place, rights are not traits of human nature, entailed by other traits, but modes of behavior, institutionalized ways in which the members of a community behave toward one another and which must be learned. Actual participation in this behavior, in rights-relations, does have prerequisites. Thus, it presupposes the fully developed ability to govern oneself by rights-norms and rules out (human) fetuses and even newborns. Even if, as the defenders of fetal rights contend, fetuses (or even fertilized human ova) are human persons, they still do not have the powers of normative self-governance or the ability to respect rights-entitlements that are exercised in rights-relations. If we consider that which benefits something as being in its interest, we can admit that fetuses have interests, as Feinberg maintains they do. Granted all of this, human fetuses are still only possible or potential rights-participants, not actual ones. It is this distinction that Feinberg, who attributes rights to future generations as well as the unborn, misses, and I think he does so because he thinks of rights as properties rather than as activities in which we engage together with others. On the other hand, the fact that normal newborns have the potentiality to develop into rights-participants is of singular importance. If they are treated as such, as having both rights-entitlements and the obligation to respect them, they will learn the attitudes and behaviors proper to those roles; they will come to internalize and govern themselves by rights-norms. For this reason they should be so treated. The learning that takes place, because it is active and not merely learning *about* rights, will result in the attitude of the community becoming part of the child's own attitude or perspective as a self.

Individualism

Individuals can have rights—i.e., rights-entitlements and rights-obligations—but they cannot have them in isolation from other individuals any more than they can have them in isolation from the communities in which those rights are institutionalized. As we have seen, a right is inherently relational and reciprocal. To "have a right" is to be involved in such a relation with others, not to have a property that belongs to one independently. Not only are the roles in a rights-relation reciprocally defined—even though in principle one has both roles, actualization of the right always presupposes a party who is entitled and one who implements the obligation to honor that entitlement; each member of the community in which the right is operative is empowered to play the one role and required to play the other whenever circumstances make either of these appropriate—but enactment of either role requires enactment of the other as its complement. Even the exercise of liberties involves respect by others; those who deny that there is any duty or obligation correlative to a liberty overlook the fact that, to be a right, a liberty must be institutionalized. What it means for a liberty to be institutionalized as a rights-entitlement is precisely that all the members of a community are obligated to refrain from interfering with it, an obligation that may be expressed in laws specifying that this liberty is to be protected. If the obligation is not recognized and accepted as such, one may be free to act in a particular way at any given time or place, but this freedom is not a right. Perhaps no one will interfere with it now, but there are no strictures against interfering with it the next time. (On the other hand, it should be noted that even if it is written into law, if the obligation to respect this freedom is not recognized and accepted in practice, no such right is operative.)

It is my contention that communities, too, can have rights; that, like individuals, at least some communities have the powers that enable them to participate in rights-relations. As we have seen, there are theorists who rule out community rights because they deny the reality of communities themselves. They see the existence of communities as posing an ontological problem because they are composed of individuals, and they therefore take them to be reducible to those individual members whom they view as independent existents (unlike an organism, which is not reducible to its component cells because they are not independent individuals). But if we accept the idea that anything that is efficacious, that in any way makes a difference, is real, communities are undoubtedly real. The attitude or perspective shared by those who regulate their interactions by it, the perspective Mead calls the attitude of a generalized other, is one means by which a community is efficacious. (I prefer the term 'perspective', which seems to me to be more inclusive than 'attitude'.) The perspective of a generalized other is not identical with the personal perspective of any single member or of them all together; produced by them jointly, it is a perspective that they share, but that is only one component of their personal perspectives. Insofar as they share it, and only insofar as they do, these individuals constitute a community, which is something over and above what they would be as isolated or independent individuals who did not share in this attitude.

Participation in rights is participation in relations with others. For a community to do this would require it to share in a perspective which was that of a wider community, a perspective that includes rights-norms; it would also require the community (and all the other members of the more inclusive community) to be able to govern itself by those norms, to respect as well as have rights-entitlements, and to express this respect in action. All of this presupposes that a community can judge and act as a body;

that it not only is efficacious in the sense specified, but can function agentially.

First of all, communities do belong to more inclusive communities, which is to say that any number of communities can have elements of their perspectives, including norms, in common. Second, any community that can produce a vote or somehow arrive at and express consensus has a voice and can participate in dialogue with others; any community whose members can generate a decision that their community is to be bound by a norm or law or decision of a more inclusive community, and any community capable of electing a representative to speak or to act in its name, is able to function as an agent. Whether by vote or (in the case of small communities) by consensus, a community can install norms extending rights to all the members of an inclusive community as components of its perspective as a community; by the same means, it can acknowledge as well as exercise entitlements, can accept the obligation to respect them and implement that respect when called upon, and can call upon other communities to do so. In so doing it is engaging in rights–relations with those other communities.

There are some communities that can participate in rights–relations with individuals. A corporation, for instance, is a particular sort of organized community, and can enter into contracts both with other corporations or communities of other kinds (a city, for instance) and with individuals (customers, clients, or suppliers, or even their own employees). Under the norms defining and governing contracts, both parties to a contract are alike entitled to have its provisions carried out and are alike obligated to do so, even though the provisions of the contract assign different specific entitlements and obligations to each. And if either were in the position of the other, it would have the other's entitlements and obligations. Every individual member of a community in which the right of contract is operative should have internalized the norms governing that right; every subcommunity of that community, companies and corporations in particular, should similarly govern itself by those norms; i.e., they should be included among the rules and principles in terms of which it operates. The norms governing the right of contract (or any comparable right) may be written into law, or stated in the manuals or other documents by

which the activities of participating subcommunities are controlled. But whether or not they are formally stated, where the
institution of contract exists, individuals and subcommunities
alike must govern themselves by the same norms.

Moreover, there are rights in which communities ought to participate. It follows from the definition of a right that no member
of a community should be denied any of the rights that are operative there. By the same definition, this applies not only to individuals but also to the subcommunities that are the members of an
inclusive community. For instance, a right of sovereignty institutionalized in a community of nation states cannot be denied to
any member of that community without negating it, without denying that it is really a right. Beyond this, to affirm a right, as
Mead can be understood to be saying, is to affirm the intention
to extend both the entitlement and the obligation to respect it to
all; so that for a right to be institutionalized is for the members of
the community in which it is operative to commit themselves to
its universalization, even if that right is not in fact (as it is unlikely
to be) universally operative. Again, this is as true for the members
of a community of communities as it is for a community of individuals. To assert the existence of a right or to claim to have a
right is to say implicitly not only that anyone who has internalized
the norms governing that right knows he or she ought to respect
it and to require others to respect it as well, but also that any
individual or any community that is similarly situated ought to
have the same right. Most important, since the necessary conditions of community are also prerequisites of the existence and
stability of a community of communities, those rights I have identified as fundamental and generic ought to be operative for all the
(sub)communities of every inclusive community. Each should be
equally entitled to participate in the affairs of that inclusive community as an autonomous and authoritative agent.

The principle that no rights should be selectively denied the
members of any community entails another sort of right, closely
related to what I am calling community rights. On my definition
of a right, no individuals should be selectively denied any rights
operative in their community or communities, so that none
should be denied the fundamental generic rights on the basis of
their membership in any particular subcommunity. That is, no

individuals should be excluded from participating in rights on the basis of their collective identity. Thus, in addition to the rights they have or ought to have as individuals, the members of every (sub)community within a wider community should have a collective entitlement to equal treatment: an entitlement to participate in all the rights accorded the members of any other subcommunity of their parent community. This right of equal treatment, which the members of each subcommunity, collectively as well as individually, are also obligated to respect, has its most significant application in the case of ethnic minorities. But it should be operative in and for every community, whatever its constitution.

NOTES

1. Wesley Newcomb Hohfeld, *Fundamental Legal Conceptions*, ed. W. W. Cook (New Haven, Connecticut: Yale University Press, 1919), p. 38.

2. Judith Jarvis Thomson, *The Realm of Rights* (Cambridge, Massachusetts: Harvard University Press, 1990), p. 41.

3. Alan Gewirth, *Human Rights: Essays on Justification and Applications* (Chicago and London: The University of Chicago Press, 1982), p. 49.

4. Joel Feinberg, "The Nature and Value of Rights," in *Rights*, ed. David Lyons (Belmont, California: Wadsworth, 1979), p. 90.

5. Virginia Held, *Rights and Goods: Justifying Social Action* (New York: The Free Press, 1984), p. 15.

6. On affirmative action, see, for example, Bernard R. Boxill, *Blacks and Social Justice* (Totowa, New Jersey: Rowman and Allanheld, 1984); Ronald Dworkin, *A Matter of Principle* (Cambridge, Massachusetts: Harvard University Press, 1985), Part Five, "Reverse Discrimination"; Gertrude Ezorsky, *Racism and Justice: The Case for Affirmative Action* (Ithaca, New York: Cornell University Press, 1991).

7. George Herbert Mead, too, speaks in terms of the obligation to respect a right rather than in terms of duties; see, for example, *Movements of Thought in the Nineteenth Century*, ed. Merritt H. Moore (Chicago: The University of Chicago Press, 1936), p. 13; hereafter cited as MT.

8. Margaret MacDonald, "Natural Rights," *Proceedings of the Aristotelian Society* (1947–48), repr. in *Theories of Rights*, ed. Jeremy Waldron (Oxford: Oxford University Press, 1989).

9. I take the term 'dialogic reciprocity' and the basic idea of a community of dialogic reciprocity from Drucilla Cornell, "Two Lectures on the Normative Dimensions of Community in the Law," second lecture, "In Defense of Dialogic Reciprocity," *Tennessee Law Review*, 54 (1987), 335–343.

3

Jean-Jacques Rousseau, John Stuart Mill, and Thomas Hill Green on Natural Rights

MOST DISCUSSIONS OF HUMAN RIGHTS, at least in the United States, take for granted the principles of natural rights theory as it emanated from the tradition of natural law and the writings of Hugo Grotius, Thomas Hobbes, and John Locke. These writers were not in complete agreement on all the relevant theses, and they were not always consistent in their doctrines, but the sediment of their views was handed down not only to Thomas Jefferson and the Founding Fathers of the United States, but also to later theorists to the present day. In the preceding pages, I discussed a number of contemporary theories of rights that diverge from this dominant school of thought. But these challenges to classical natural rights theory have significant antecedents. Preeminent among those whose theories contradict it are Jean-Jacques Rousseau, John Stuart Mill, and Thomas Hill Green, with whom this chapter will be concerned. While they all reject the concept of "natural rights" in the classical sense, Rousseau, Mill, and Green have given us theories of rights that are naturalistic, in the sense that they are grounded in these philosophers' respective analyses of empirically observable human behavior and motivation.

To begin with, what is meant by "natural rights"? Those rights taken to be universal (as opposed to "special" rights relevant to specific circumstances) were held by the classical theorists to be natural in at least four interrelated senses. The first is that they are innate, not conventional or socially conferred. Whether these rights are said to be God-given or not, all humans, simply *as* human, are endowed with them. That is, rights are "natural to man" in the sense of being inseparable from our being, just in virtue of our humanity. (This is the view I call 'essentialism'.) And they are "natural" in the further sense of being knowable by reason, *a priori*, just as reason discovers the natural law. In this sense, traditional natural rights theories, even those of Hobbes and Locke, are appropriately said to be rationalist.[1]

Those who conceive rights in this way assume that we have them, as we each possess human nature, not only as humans, but as human *individuals*.[2] Even the American Declaration of Independence, which starts by mentioning the necessity for a *people* to "dissolve the political bands, which have connected them with another," and to "assume . . . separate and equal status," justifies this action by appeal to the "self-evident" truth, not that all *peoples* "are created equal," but that "all *men*" are. Natural rights theories, that is, are overwhelmingly individualist.[3] Typically, their individualism takes a stronger form as well, the form characterized in Chapter 1 as atomism. They hold rights to belong to individuals taken independently rather than as members of society. This atomistic view is logically connected to the essentialist notion that we possess rights in virtue of our human nature, a nature that each of us possesses as an individual. The same essentialist assumption also entails the universalism of the natural rights view. Entailed by and inseparable from human nature, rights necessarily belong to all humans. But partly because of the history of the concept and theory of rights—rights were originally thought of as protection against the arbitrary exercise of governmental power—and partly because of the atomistic individualism in terms of which the concept was framed, rights came to be thought of in adversarial terms. Thus, individuals are said to have rights *against* not only government, but other individuals. Each of the theories I shall discuss departs from one or more of these assumptions.

JEAN-JACQUES ROUSSEAU

Despite inconsistencies in his writings, the dominant thrust of Rousseau's treatment of rights clearly runs counter to the theory of natural rights as he encountered it. Neither law nor rights, according to him, are natural in the sense of being either antecedent to society or inherent in original human nature. In the introductory section of his *Discourse on the Origin of Inequality,* he states its objective: "Precisely what, then, is the subject of this discourse? To mark, in the progress of things, the moment when, right taking the place of violence, nature was subjected to the law."[4] Arguing, in his *Social Contract,* that "the social order is a sacred right which serves as a basis for all others," he nevertheless maintains that even this right "does not come from nature; it is therefore based on conventions."[5] Rights, for him, neither are innate nor belong to individuals prior to or outside the framework of society. They arise and have their sphere of operation within society, and society itself is a human artifact, the product of a compact, although one that is sharply different from those posited by Hobbes and Locke.[6]

Not only does he see rights to be products of society rather than inherent traits of human nature, but Rousseau also denies that human nature, at least as scholars had come to think of it, is innate. In the first version of the *Contract,* criticizing an article on natural law by Diderot (a critique excluded from the final draft), he writes, "we begin properly to become men only after we have become citizens."[7] But being human is not just a matter of becoming political beings. Man was long defined as rational, but, according to Rousseau, even reason, depending on language for its development, is not an innate human characteristic: "All the kinds of knowledge that demand reflection, all those acquired only by the concatenation of ideas and perfected only successively, appear to be utterly beyond the grasp of savage man, owing to the lack of communication with his fellow-men, that is to say, owing to the lack of the instrument which is used for that communication . . ." (DOI 74n6).[8]

The contract that constitutes the social order—and turns "savage" men into humans as we know them—establishes the framework for rights and determines their nature and function. Accepting the proposition that survival of the human race is impossible in the natural state (in which each individual attempts to maintain himself), he contends that men require "a form of association which defends and protects with the whole force of the community the person and goods of every associate, and by means of which each, uniting with all, nevertheless obeys only himself and remains as free as before" (SC 14). As conceived by

Rousseau, the social contract does not, as the Hobbesian contract does, simply transfer all power and control to a sovereign ruler; it consists, instead, in the generation of a common will that has authority over all. As he himself puts it, the compact "reduces itself to the following terms: *Each of us puts in common his person and his whole power under the supreme direction of the general will; and in return we receive in a body every member as an indivisible part of the whole*" (SC 15). Sovereignty, which has to be understood as moral authority, is "only the exercise of the general will" (SC 23). Government is its agent.

By establishing sovereign authority, in principle identical with that of each of the citizens, the social contract establishes what Rousseau terms "moral society." The existence of the general will makes it possible for society to legislate duties that every citizen, being their author—the source of their authority—as well as their subject, will take to be binding not only upon himself but also upon all the others. Not only is this principle the basis of morality; but, as we shall see, it is central to Rousseau's portrayal of rights.

After the contract, Rousseau has said, we remain free as before. The freedom or liberty that has been retained, however, has undergone a transformation. No longer merely the power of action, it has now been authorized, legitimated. By the social contract man loses "his natural liberty" and gains "civil liberty," and "we must clearly distinguish natural liberty, which is limited only by the force of the individual, from civil liberty, which is limited by the general will" (SC 18). "Limited" must be understood here, not in the sense of being bounded or restricted by external forces, but in the sense of being proportional to enabling conditions; we enjoy civil liberty insofar as it is guaranteed by civil authority rather than brute strength.

Property, like civil liberty, also comes into existence with civil society. By the social contract, Rousseau says, man loses "an unlimited right to anything which tempts him and which he is able to attain" and gains "the ownership of all that he possesses"; and he goes on to distinguish "possession, which is only the result of force or the right of the first occupant, from ownership which can only be based on a positive title" (SC 18–19). The phraseology here seems to imply the existence of a "natural" right, antecedent to civil society. In a previous paragraph, too, he has characterized the contract in terms of "the total alienation of each associate, with all of his rights, to the whole community" (SC 14). Is Rousseau contradicting himself and accepting the existence of natural rights antecedent to society?

Other passages show that this is not his intent. At the start of Chapter 8 of Book I of the *Contract* he says, "This passage from the state of nature to the civil state produces in man a very remarkable change, by substituting in his conduct justice for instinct, and by giving his actions the morality that they previously lacked." It is only then, he continues, that "right succeeds appetite" (SC 18). And in Chapter 3, "The Right of the Strongest," he discusses the word 'right':

> The strongest man is never strong enough to be always master unless he transforms his force into right, and obedience into duty. Hence the right of the strongest—a right assumed ironically in appearance, and really established in principle. But will this word never be explained to us? Force is a physical power; I do not see what morality can result from its effects. To yield to force is an act of necessity, not of will; it is at most an act of prudence. In what sense could it be a duty?
>
> Let us suppose for a moment this pretended right. I say that nothing results from it but an inexplicable muddle. For as soon as force constitutes right, . . . every force which overcomes the first succeeds to its right [privilege]. . . . But what sort of a right perishes when force ceases [SC 7]?

The supposed natural rights of liberty and property, then, are only "pretended" rights, "rights" in quotation marks. Genuine rights, like duties, can exist only in moral society, and moral society is civil society—a social and political order into which human beings enter and which they create, not a preexisting "natural" order governed only by force.

As noted in the previous chapters, the American philosopher George Herbert Mead, discussing the background of nineteenth-century philosophic thought, called attention to the central feature of Rousseau's analysis of rights and incorporated it into his own thinking. This is the principle that rights are reciprocal or mutual, a principle that rests directly on the way Rousseau portrays the social contract. As early as the *Discourse on Inequality*, Rousseau had linked "the true foundations of the body politic" and "the reciprocal rights of its members" (DOI 14). In the *Contract*, he says, "The engagements which bind us to the social body are obligatory only because they are mutual, and their nature is such that in fulfilling them we cannot work for others without also working for ourselves" (SC 28). Rights are similarly mutual. In entering into the compact, "each, in giving himself to all, gives himself to nobody; and . . . there is not one associate over whom we do not acquire the same rights which we concede to him over ourselves . . ." (SC 14). This mutuality is one with the principle of equal rights and the right of all citizens to equality as such. The contract creates a will that is general, not only in being the product of the wills of all who constitute it, but in its content: "the general will, to be truly such, must be just in its object as in its essence." Not only must it "proceed from all," and "be applicable to all," but the general will must legislate universally: "it loses its natural rectitude when it is directed to some individual and determinate object, because in that case . . . we have no true principle of equity to guide us" (SC 28–29).

This is to say that, rather than serving a selected interest, the general will must express a common interest, one in which individual interests are equally realized. For this to be actualized in practice, as it is where all are understood to have rights and accept the duty to respect them, requires that the citizens perceive the relation. "Equality of rights and the notion of justice that it produces," Rousseau tells us, "derive from the preference that each gives himself."[9] This is possible only if each of us understands that, all being similarly motivated, for anyone to have rights, all must respect the rights of each, and each the rights of all.

The model of rights, for Rousseau, is legal rights. For instance, at the close of Book I of the *Contract*, he states that "the fundamental pact . . . substitutes a moral and legitimate equality for the physical inequality which nature imposed upon men, so that, although unequal in strength or talent, they all become equal by convention and legal right" (SC 22–23). And in the section on the law in Book II, he says, "in the civil state . . . all the rights are fixed by the law" (SC 34). This is important not only because he holds the law to be a decree of "the whole people," but also because it "considers the subjects in a body and the actions as abstract, never a man as an individual nor a particular action" (SC

34–35). Morality is general and transcends individual difference. This is the import of his statement, quoted above, that the general will "loses its natural rectitude when it is directed to some individual and determinate object, because in that case . . . we have no true principle of equity to guide us" (SC 28–29).

Summarizing his reading of Rousseau's thesis, Mead says: "rights exist only in so far as they are acknowledged, and only to the extent that those who claim them acknowledge them in the person of others. No man can claim a right who does not at the same time affirm his own obligation to respect that right in all others."[10] This principle expresses the form of the general will. Rights such as those of liberty, property, and equality must be respected as well as held by all the citizens because each is at once legislating to and obeying himself as well as all the others. Being legislated or, as Rousseau says, based on "conventions," rights cannot be innate; and embodying the mutuality of the contract, rights are common and mutual, not private, possessions. That is, Rousseau rejects the thesis of atomistic individualism as well; and even though he occasionally speaks of rights "against" others, he makes it clear that if it is a genuine right, both (or all) parties must have it and must respect it in one another. Thus, in the sense that he sees us to hold them jointly rather than at one another's expense, he is denying that rights are adversarial. And as features of political society and the compact on which it rests, in opposition to the theses of essentialism and rationalism, rights are neither entailed by human nature nor knowable by reason *a priori*.

JOHN STUART MILL

It is in *Utilitarianism* that Mill discusses the nature and ground of rights, which he introduces in order to show the difference between morality in general and justice. His approach is empirical. Utilizing the then current terminology of "perfect" and "imperfect" obligation, Mill holds the difference to be that "duties of perfect obligation are those duties in virtue of which a correlative *right* resides in some person or persons," whereas "duties of imperfect obligation are those moral obligations which do not give birth to any right." The former define the sphere of justice.[11] He goes on to define a right as follows:

> When we call anything a person's right, we mean that he has a valid claim on society to protect him in the possession of it, either by the force of law or by that of education and opinion. If he has what we consider a sufficient claim, on whatever account, to have something guaranteed to him by society, we say that he has a right to it [U 52].[12]

Rights, here, are not necessarily legal rights but include what we call moral rights. But even those that are not codified, rather than being innate or grounded in human nature, are determined by human judgment, by "what we consider a sufficient claim, on whatever account" (U 52). On what grounds do we judge that the claim is sufficient? What determines its validity? "To have a right . . . is, I conceive, to have something which society ought to defend me in the possession of. If the objector goes on to ask why it ought, I can give him no other reason than general utility" (U 52).

If this is so, then what is the peculiar utility of that which we take to be a right as compared with any other obligation? Mill turns to psychology for the answer. The question is, what are the constitutents of "the sentiment of justice"—what we today call the *sense* of justice—and why is it stronger than moral feelings in general? The answer will tell us why we take the obligation to respect a right to be so strong, stronger than other moral obligations—in the older language, to be a perfect rather than an imperfect obligation, or, as some say today, why rights are "trumps."

The sentiment of justice, Mill tells us, has three components. He states them in several ways, but essentially they are our need for security, the thirst for retaliation when we have been harmed, and the feeling of sympathy with others who have been harmed. It is the social sympathies that convert the personal interest in security and desire for vengeance into a moral concern. What we mean when we speak of "the violation of a right" is that an injustice has been done; and what we mean by this is that we feel that a specific wrong to a particular person demands punishment: "a hurt to some assignable person or persons, on the one hand, and a demand for punishment on the other. An examination of our own minds, I think, will show that these two things include all that we mean when we speak of the violation of a right" (U 52).

The reason we feel this way, and the reason we take the wrong to be not merely a hurt but one that society should punish and protect us from, are that the wrong in question threatens "the most vital" of all our interests, the interest in security, something that "no human being can possibly do without."

> Our notion, therefore, of the claim we have on our fellow creatures to join in making safe for us the very groundwork of our existence gathers feelings around it so much more intense than those concerned in any of the more common cases of utility that the difference in degree (as is often the case in psychology) becomes a real difference in kind. . . . The feelings concerned are so powerful, and we count so positively on finding a responsive feeling in others (all being alike interested), that *ought* and *should* grow into *must*, and recognized indispensability becomes a moral necessity . . . [U 53].

Rights, then, while they are not inherent in or entailed by human nature as such, are products of empirically discoverable psychological tendencies, including the interest of all in protection by society. "Now this most indispensable of all necessaries, after physical nutriment"—that is, security—"cannot be had unless the machinery for providing it is kept unintermittedly in active play" (U 53). Apart from society, individuals cannot have rights.

Mill rejects the essentialist thesis along with those of innateness and atomicity, and, as an empiricist, he finds the rationalist approach and assumptions to be totally foreign. Concerning the view that laws governing human behavior are "self-evident and self-justifying," he says in the introductory section of *On Liberty*, "This all but universal illusion is one of the examples of the magical influence of custom, which is not only, as the proverb says, a second nature but is continually mistaken for the first."[13] Rather than discoveries of reason, rights are established by people because they are found, in experience, to be necessary prerequisites of social life: ". . . the fact of living in society renders it indispensable that each should be bound to observe a certain line of conduct toward the rest. This conduct consists, first, in not injuring the interests of one another, or rather certain interests which, either by express legal provision or by tacit understanding, ought to be considered as rights. . . ."[14]

THOMAS HILL GREEN

Writing toward the end of the nineteenth century, T. H. Green emphatically rejected the classical concept of natural rights. " 'Natural right'," he said, "as = right in a state of nature which is not a state of society, is a contradiction."[15] Nevertheless, he was not willing to limit rights to those that are enforced by law. "[T]here are no rights antecedent to society," he insists (PPO 47),

> but it does not follow from this that there is not a true and important sense in which natural rights and obligations exist—the same sense as that in which duties exist, though unfulfilled. There is a system of rights and obligations which *should be* maintained by law, whether it is so or not, and which may properly be called 'natural', not in the sense in which the term 'natural' would imply that such a system ever did exist or could exist independently of force exercised by society over individuals, but 'natural' because necessary to the end which it is the vocation of human society to realise [PPO 33–34].

The end to whose achievement Green sees rights to be necessary is the "fulfilment . . . of a moral capacity without which a man would not be a man" (PPO 47). But it is not the bare fact of having this capacity—its being an essential trait of human nature—that accounts for rights, that establishes their "naturalness." Green thought of human nature, not as an essence exemplified by all humans, but as the ideal fulfillment of the potentialities that typify the species, an idea he derived from Aristotle and Hegel.[16] The moral capacity justifies certain rights because those rights are prerequisites of its exercise.

> The capacity . . . on the part of the individual of conceiving a good as the same for himself and others, and of being determined to action by that conception, is the foundation of rights; and rights are the condition of that capacity being realized. No right is justifiable or should be a right except on the ground that directly or indirectly it serves this purpose. Conversely . . . society should secure to the

individual every power, that is necessary for realising this capacity
[PPO 47].

That is, the capacity for identifying one's own interest or good
with that of others is a necessary condition of rights, which are,
in turn, a necessary condition for that capacity to be operative in
society. But what is the sufficient condition for the *existence* of
rights?

To exist, rights must be recognized: "rights are made by recognition." They exist in the consciousness of those who are ready
to determine their behavior by that consciousness, this readiness
"resting on the recognition . . . of each other as determined, or
capable of being determined, by the conception of a common
good" (PPO 140–141). And, he continues, "There is no right
but thinking makes it so—none that is not derived from some
idea that men have about each other. Nothing is more real than a
right, yet its existence is purely ideal, if by 'ideal' is meant that
which is not dependent on anything material but has its being
solely in consciousness" (PPO 141).

For rights to exist, then, is for people not only to conceive
them, but also to understand them to serve a common good that
each conceives as his own and that each therefore acts to promote.
"The capacity to conceive a common good as one's own and to
regulate the exercise of one's powers by reference to a good
which others recognise, carries with it the consciousness that
powers *should be* so exercised; which means that there *should be*
rights, that powers should be regulated by mutual recognition"
(PPO 45). And again: "There can be no right without a consciousness of common interest on the part of members of a society. Without this there might be certain powers on the part of
individuals, but no recognition of these powers by others as powers of which they allow the exercise, nor any claim to such recognition; and without this recognition or claim to recognition there
can be no right" (PPO 48).[17]

In short, to will the end is to will the means, and to understand
this is both to understand that certain rights, such as the right to
"free life," that is, liberty, and to "the instruments of such life,"
that is, property, ought to exist and to justify that existence (PPO
216–217). Members of society who conceive "an ideal good" that

is the same for all of them will regard any power whose exercise is a means to that good "as one which should be exercised." And "the free exercise of his powers is secured to each member through the recognition by each of the others as entitled to the same freedom with himself" (PPO 44). This is to say that freedom to exercise any of the powers in question is assured only if it is a right; and it is made a right by mutual entitlement. The atomistic conception of rights as properties of independent individuals, antecedent to membership in society, is ruled out. Not only are rights dependent on social recognition; but, rather than being asserted by individuals, adversarially, in opposition to one another or society, they are understood by Green, much as they are by Rousseau, to be mutually conferred by the members of a society upon one another, and the connotation of a general will is deliberate: "It is only as within a society, as a relation between its members, though the society be that of all men, that there can be such a thing as a right; and the right to free life rests on the common will of the society, in the sense that each member of the society within which the right subsists in seeking to satisfy himself contributes to satisfy the others, and that each is aware that the other does so; whence there results a common interest in the free play of the powers of all" (PPO 216).

Green is asserting that rights are and must be products not only of society, but of a self-conscious society: of persons cognizant of a common interest and of sharing this awareness, and therefore willing, as well as able, jointly to regulate their behavior. He firmly denies that rights can be innate in the sense of inborn or that of being traits of an essential, antecedently "given" human nature. They are "innate," he says, only in the "Aristotelian" sense that they "arise out of, and are necessary for the fulfillment of, a moral capacity without which a man would not be a man" (PPO 47). This capacity, which is the capacity to determine oneself by what one understands to be a common good, is what enables humans to be moral beings. While he has been influenced by Kant, as well as by Hegel, Green is not saying that rights are dictated or directly entailed by moral nature as such. He is saying that because we are potentially moral beings, because we can understand that in order to realize our own ideal end we must realize that of society, we can see the necessity and the importance of rights and are consequently capable of establishing and respecting them. Exercise of this moral capacity, therefore, is both means and end: it is a necessary means for the realization of a common good; and, being the fulfillment of a distinctive human capacity, an ideal end for each of us as well as for society as a whole. "The moral capacity implies a consciousness on the part of the subject of the capacity that its realisation is an end desirable in itself, and rights are the condition of realising it. Only through the possession of rights can the power of the individual freely to make a common good his own have reality given to it" (PPO 45).

The realization that the moral capacity is an end desirable in itself is a realization that, the common good being part of and a necessary condition of our own, individual good, exercise of this capacity is part of and serves our own interest. "There ought to be rights, because the moral personality—the capacity on the part of an individual for making a common good his own—ought to be developed; and it is developed through rights; i.e., through the recognition by members of a society of powers in each other contributory to a common good and the regulation of those powers by that recognition" (PPO 45).

The Hegelian strain in Green's thinking is strong here. We are motivated by a conscious ideal of ourselves, one that is inseparable from an ideal of society. "[R]ights are derived from the possession of personality as = a rational will (or the capacity which man possesses of being determined to action by the conception of such a perfection of his being as involves the perfection of a society in which he lives) . . ." (PPO 46). However, I do not think Green's theory of rights stands or falls with the assertion that we have a conception of the "perfection" of our being, an assertion I do not find to be verifiable. The existence of a "rational" or moral will, in the sense of one that is motivated by "a consciousness of common interest on the part of members of a society" (PPO 48), is sufficient to show that we can see rights as serving that interest and, therefore, serving our own. This perception serves as the ground for the mutual recognition of rights by those who, if Green, Mill, and Rousseau are correct, must be seen as jointly conferring them.

NOTES

1. "[N]atural Reason . . . tells us, that men, being once born, have a right to their preservation, and consequently to meat and drink, and such other things as nature affords for their subsistence" (John Locke, *Two Treatises of Government*, ed. Peter Laslett [Cambridge: Cambridge University Press, 1963], Second Treatise, Chapter 5, p. 303). On the name 'rationalism', see A. P. d'Entrèves, *Natural Law: An Historical Survey* (London: Hutchinson University Library, 1951; repr. New York: Harper Torchbooks, 1965), p. 49.

2. Rights attributed to governments, to the state or sovereign, are not, strictly speaking, rights of individuals, but, as in Hobbes, the sovereign is treated as an individual, even if it is an assembly, and governments are said to have rights *over* individuals.

3. George H. Sabine summarizes Locke's individualism as follows: "Instead of a law enjoining the common good of a society, Locke set up a body of innate, indefeasible, individual rights which limit the competence of the community and stand as bars to prevent interference with the liberty and property of private persons" (*A History of Political Theory* [New York: Henry Holt, 1950], p. 529).

4. Jean-Jacques Rousseau, *Discourse on the Origin of Inequality* (1755), trans. Donald A. Cress (Indianapolis: Hackett, 1962), pp. 16–17; hereafter cited as DOI.

5. Jean-Jacques Rousseau, *Of the Social Contract, or, Principles of Political Right* (1762), trans. Charles M. Sherover (New York: Harper & Row, 1984), p. 4; hereafter cited as SC.

6. The only natural form of society, as Rousseau sees it, is the family, and it endures only as long as the children's dependence upon their father (SC 4).

7. Jean-Jacques Rousseau, *Contrat social*, first version, Chapter 2, in *Political Writings of Jean-Jacques Rousseau* I, ed. C. E. Vaughan (Cambridge: Cambridge University Press, 1915), quoted in Sabine, *History of Political Theory*, p. 582.

8. The only "operations of the human soul" that seem to be prior to reason Rousseau identifies as those underlying self-interest or self-love (which, in the notes, he distinguishes from egocentrism), and what we would call sympathy (which he distinguishes from an instinct of sociality).

9. ". . . and consequently," he continues, "from man's nature . . ." (SC 28). In the *Discourse on Inequality*, however, he makes it plain that when he talks of "human nature" he does not mean human nature as

we encounter it, fully developed, in society. (See previous note and the discussion of reason below.)

10. George Herbert Mead, *Movements of Thought in the Nineteenth Century*, ed. Merritt H. Moore (Chicago: The University of Chicago Press, 1936), p. 13. Mead seems to suggest that this principle underlies, rather than rests on, the authority of the general will. For reasons already stated, I disagree with this, as well as with his assertion that Rousseau found the basis for the institutions of society in "man's rational nature."

11. John Stuart Mill, *Utilitarianism* (1861), ed. George Sher (Indianapolis: Hackett, 1979), p. 48; hereafter cited as U.

12. Mill has been construed here as sharing the assumption of the natural rights theorists that people have at least some rights that are not dependent on society. See, for example, Rex Martin, *A System of Rights* (Oxford: Clarendon Press, 1993), p. 51 and note 3. I believe the additional passages I shall quote indicate otherwise.

13. John Stuart Mill, *On Liberty* (1859), ed. Elizabeth Rapaport (Indianapolis: Hackett, 1978), p. 5.

14. Ibid., p. 90.

15. Thomas Hill Green, *Lectures on the Principles of Political Obligation and Other Writings*, ed. Paul Harris and John Morrow (Cambridge: Cambridge University Press, 1968), p. 48; hereafter cited as PPO. Green's lectures were published posthumously.

16. "Indeed, the whole moral ideal of self-realization of the Idealists, combined with a secondary recognition of the place of self-interest and pleasure, is fundamentally Aristotelian, however filtered through Hegel's adaptation" (John Herman Randall, Jr., "Idealistic Social Philosophy and Bernard Bosanquet," *Philosophy and Phenomenological Research*, 26, No. 4 [June 1966]; repr. in John Herman Randall, Jr., *Philosophy After Darwin: Chapters for The Career of Philosophy, Volume III, and Other Essays*, ed. Beth J. Singer [New York: Columbia University Press, 1977], pp. 98–99).

17. I do not find Sir David Ross's criticism of Green on the issue of recognition to be well taken: "Now it is plainly wrong to describe either legal or moral rights as depending for their existence on their recognition, for to recognize a thing (in the sense in which 'recognize' is here used) is to recognize it as existing already" (*The Right and the Good* [Oxford: Clarendon Press, 1930]), appendix to Chapter 2; repr. in *Readings in Ethical Theory*, ed. Wilfrid Sellars and John Hospers [New York: Appleton-Century-Crofts, 1952], p. 199). The sense of "recognition" here is not that in which we recognize an identity we already knew. It is recognition in the sense of sanctioning, closer to the sense in which one who is chairing a meeting "recognizes" someone who wishes to speak,

authorizing that person to do so. For the members of society to "recognize" an action as a right is for them to "allow" its exercise, to authorize it. Ross also errs in attributing to Green the view that the existence of a right depends upon the recognition of the "power" in question in the one supposed to have that right—a distortion and oversimplification of Green's claim that the human capacity for awareness of a common interest is a necessary condition of the social recognition of rights.

II
DEMOCRACY AND MULTICULTURALISM

4

The Democratic Solution to Ethnic Pluralism*

THE GENERAL THESIS OF THIS CHAPTER is not only that minority rights are compatible with political unity, but also that they are a means to and a necessary condition of that unity. There is an obvious defense of this thesis: minorities who are denied rights will fight for them, and the result will be turmoil in the wider society. But I shall defend the thesis on grounds drawn from my own theory of rights, which I shall briefly review.

COMMUNITIES

The key concept in my theory of rights is that of community, and I use this word in a special way. In the most general sense, a community is any collection of persons who, usually because of some common condition or parallel experience, share a perspective, a point of view or attitude that conditions the way they respond to things or situations of some kind. The significance of this kind of community is that having a common perspective makes communication possible. Consider the understanding glances exchanged at the moment of take-off among persons who share a fear of flying—a common perspective; we might say there is a *state* of community among them, in virtue of which they constitute a community: a segment of the extended community of all who share the same fear. For community in this generic sense, I use the name 'perspectival community'. If community is commonality of perspective, then communities with some aspect of their perspectives in common constitute a community of communities, an inclusive community.

---

*Invited presentation, Conference on Ethnic Minorities in the Carpathian Region, Szigetvár, Hungary, October 21–23, 1992.

Among the perspectives that define communities are those we call social norms: the shared understandings, expectations, rules of behavior, goals and interests, values and concerns, and so forth that enable us to communicate and interact with one another in a meaningful way and characterize us as social beings. All those who have internalized a common set of norms constitute what I call a 'normative community'. Lecturers and those who attend lectures, for example, having internalized the norms governing such activities, belong to this kind of community, as do all who speak the same language and all who know how to read a map. Each of us belongs to indefinitely many communities, large and small, organized and unorganized, some more and some less central to our sense of self and of our own identity. Communities overlap and intersect in indefinitely many ways, and a given community (or segment thereof) may be a subcommunity of any number of more inclusive communities. Communities need not be localized. The intellectual community, its subcommunity of historians, typify communities that transcend geographic and linguistic boundaries and are dispersed through many other communities. Very important to most of us are the cultural or ethnic communities to which we belong and with which we tend to identify strongly. These communities or segments of them typically are subcommunities of political communities, that is, states or nations.

Ethnic identity is often called 'nationality', but in English this word is used ambiguously, and ethnicity needs to be clearly distinguished from statehood. Members of an ethnic community are united by a cultural perspective—a tradition: a complex of norms that may be independent of political organization as well as of geography. A state or country is an organized community—inevitably a community of communities—that has a political structure as well as a unifying perspective, if only that provided by the experience of inclusion in that political entity. Due to the vicissitudes of history, virtually every territorial or political state includes diverse ethnic communities, each likely to be a segment of a wider community with additional segments in other states. Far from being a form of "false consciousness," ethnic identity is an important bond of community and a genuine and powerful component of individual identity and selfhood. While it is linked to family histories, as a cultural heritage ethnicity is not dependent on biological inheritance. Whether an ethnic subcommunity is considered to be or is treated as a minority (or is recognized as a community at all) is primarily a function of the distribution of power in the wider community. Romanians as well as Hungarians, Saxons, and Gypsies are subcommunities of the civic or political community that is Romania. Even the warring factions of what once was Yugoslavia constitute an inclusive community not only in virtue of their shared perspective as members of the formerly united state, but because their very conflict is governed by a shared, historically evolved perspective of mutual distrust, hostility, jealousy, and fear, in terms of which they relate to one another and interpret one another's behavior.

RIGHTS

Rights are usually thought of as properties—powers or immunities, liberties or entitlements—of individuals, and as belonging or adhering to them prior to membership in any community. And, as noted earlier, when their relational dimension is considered, rights are usually taken to be adversarial: claims against other persons or against society.[1] Also, despite the existence of "states' rights" in the United States, until the rights of peoples and families were enshrined by the United Nations in the Universal Declaration of Human Rights, not much attention was paid to the question whether communities, as well as individuals, could have rights. Before we can consider this question, we need to be clear what it is we are talking about when we speak of rights.

To begin with, the legalist notion of rights as inherently adversarial, however deeply entrenched, is a distortion.[2] As George Herbert Mead reminds us, even though someone's having a right imposes duties upon others, if only the duty not to violate it, rights are mutual. When we assert a right, not only are we calling upon others to acknowledge it; but the fact that we assert it *as* a right, not simply as a demand, means that "we are ready to take that same attitude toward somebody else if he makes the [same] appeal."[3] This attitude governs the institution of rights; for us to share it is for there to be "a community of attitudes which control the attitudes of all." Mead calls this community of attitudes "the attitude of the generalized other."[4] I call it the 'normative perspective' of a community.

Wherever the institution of rights exists, everyone is expected to have internalized the controlling perspective, so that when any of them asserts or claims a right he or she will evoke the prescribed response to that claim not only in others but also in him- or herself. The normative perspective encompasses both the attitude of one who claims the right and that of one who recognizes and respects it as such. Anyone who has internalized this general perspective is able, when someone asserts a right, to adopt that person's perspective, to "take the attitude of the other," and, in taking this attitude, know what this other is calling on them or some other respondent to do. Both of them know the meaning of the statement or gesture employed in asserting a right and, understanding the assertion as a rights-claim, they also know (and expect one another to know) that one who asserts an operative right is entitled to do so and that the respondent ought to honor this entitlement. And both parties understand as well that the situation would be the same were their positions reversed.

To "have a right," then, is to belong to a community whose norms prescribe and define this particular right as one that anybody may assert and that everyone is to recognize and to honor. The norms may or may not be written into law; what is important is that they are efficacious in the control of people's behavior. Contrary to natural rights theory, rights, as social institutions, are not inherent in human persons or antecedent to their membership in society. Moreover, they are not properly understood as belonging to individuals per se, because they are intrinsically relational. There are two positions or roles involved in the rights-relation, that of entitlement (to do, have, or receive the treatment that the norms prescribe) and that of being obligated to respect that entitlement. Strictly speaking, it is the entitlement and the obligation together that constitute the right. What is ordinarily called a 'right' is an entitlement: not any entitlement whatever, but one to which there is a correlative obligation of respect. I shall continue to use the conventional phraseology only when the context makes it clear that what is intended by 'right' is an entitlement. Where it does not, I shall speak of rights-entitlements. Not only do these entail reciprocal obligations, but the norms establishing a right also confer both the entitlement and the obligation to respect it (and to implement that obligation when appropriate) upon all members of the community alike. This is to say that every member of a normative community in which a right is operative stands in both positions, has both roles. And the rights-relation is reflexive as well as mutual: to have the general perspective governing a right is both to understand that one has a rights-entitlement oneself and to know that others do, and to have the same attitude of respect for one's own right as for that of others.

In principle and by definition, rights are relevant to everyone in any community in which they are operative: all participate in those rights, all have the entitlements as well as the correlative obligations, even though they are applicable only when the conditions for their implementation are satisfied. Given this, to selectively deny an operative rights-entitlement to a particular member or members of a community is not only to violate the norms, but also to deny that there is such a right—to deny that anyone has such a rights-entitlement, including oneself.

COMMUNITY RIGHTS

Rights exist only in communities, and only in those with operative rights-norms. But can communities themselves have rights? Most theories of rights assign rights only to individuals, on the ground that only they are agents or moral agents. But people are discriminated against and deprived of rights not only as individuals, but also on the basis of their collective identity, and communities as such are subjugated and even willfully destroyed, as has happened in Yugoslavia in the name of "ethnic cleansing." Can there be no rights to which they can appeal? For communities to participate in the institution of rights would require that they be able to respect one another's rights-entitlements and hold one another obligated to do so. Careful examination reveals that they can.

Communities can belong to more inclusive communities and, conversely, can also incorporate subcommunities. An inclusive community—a community of communities—is a normative one when the perspectives of its constituent communities include a common set of norms and there are norms governing relations among communities, such as the relations between Church and State, to which both are expected to conform. But what can it mean for communities as such (in contradistinction to their members) to govern themselves by social norms, by rights-norms in particular, and by what means can a community act so as to implement those norms? Can communities make judgments and perform actions? Can they function agentially?

Judging and acting are ordinarily assumed to be individual behaviors; when we speak of the actions or judgments of a community of persons—e.g., a performance by an orchestra or the verdict of a jury—can we be referring to the actions and judgments of that community as an entity or unit? Or must we, as many philosophers and sociologists claim we must, understand them to be reducible to those of individual members? Surely not the latter. In performing, the players are communicating, synchronizing and varying their playing in response to one another. The performance is a joint product, not a collection of independent ones. The deliberations of a jury are similarly mutually responsive; the verdict, a joint product. Now, consider the norms that govern such communicative interaction. Even though they involve actions and judgments by individuals, and even though they are operative only through internalization and application by individuals, social norms are genuinely products of communities.

Even though norms may remain implicit, they are judgments—prescriptive judgments. They evolve as people respond to one another's behavior and expressions, commonly in the effort to coordinate their behavior in a situation in which they are all involved or all working toward a common goal. In this process, they jointly arrive at ways of doing things and at shared understandings, assumptions, and expectations in terms of which they come to govern their own behavior and interpret that of one another. These cannot be simply the collected independent judgments of the participants, because, in order to interact and communicate meaningfully, besides being able to anticipate and predict the behavior of any of the others, each must be able to know what any of those others expects of him- or herself. This is possible only if they all come to share a perspective in and by which all the mutually responsive judgments and behaviors, all the appropriate gestures and their relevance, are prescriptively determined and can be understood. Such a generalized perspective can be the joint product only of individuals mutually engaged in a common enterprise. Even norms that, like those governing a language or other widespread social practice, have become independent of the community in which they originally evolved and are operative in an extended community originate in this way. Norms evolve in a dialogic process *and are the product of that dialogue*—hence, of the community of persons engaged in it.

Furthermore, norms are perpetuated over time and can be so only by means of successive acts of judgment. Even if they were not irreducibly communal products, norms that are transmitted to successive generations cannot be reducible to the judgments initially involved in their establishment. Whether or not they have changed, the norms that are operative at any given time are the *cumulative* product of the judgments of all who have participated in their evolution or their perpetuation, i.e., of communities as they have evolved through time.

If social norms are conjoint judgments, then any community in which there are operative norms—that is, any existing normative community—has, in fact, made such judgments and, since it can perpetuate or modify its norms, it has the power to make further judgments. However, for an inclusive community to evolve norms governing the communities that are its members, and for those members to implement these norms, each must be able to act *as* a community. Such communal agency is illustrated by the orchestra, the jury, and by a legislature when it passes a law. We speak (appropriately) of 'acts of legislation' or 'the action of the legislature'. Legislative bodies generally operate by the principle of majority rule. Even though the deciding factor in determining whether the legislation passes or not is the number of voting members by which the majority exceeds the minority, it is the vote as a whole that has legislative force. This vote is an action of the legislature as a body, as a community. The operation of the principle of majority rule gives this community a single *voice*, renders it *articulate*, enables it to act as a unit rather than as a collection of individual agents. The act of legislation expresses "the will" of the legislative body and carries its authority; through such actions this body exercises power. Moreover, through the electoral process, the legislature represents and bears the authority of a political community, and through it this community is also acting.

Like individuals, communities can also act by conferring authority on persons or groups to act in their name. By means of the media of mass communication and the application of technology to the electoral process this is increasingly possible today even for very large and widespread communities. The United States can act as a community to elect a president, and nations can form a supranational community such as the European Community or the United Nations and, through designated representatives, interact with one another and generate decisions, laws, and actions that are those of the whole community of nations. Laws, when they are actually operative, are norms, and, when nations regulate their internal governance and relations with one another by international law, they are governing themselves by social norms, operative in and through their internal governance structures and legal systems. United Nations Covenants now include laws conferring rights upon "peoples," ethnic communities. It remains to make these into operative norms. However, not all operative rights are or need to be written into law. The customs, as well as the laws, of any inclusive community can include those that prescribe respect for rights-entitlements, both of its constituent communities and of other communities with which it is bound in more inclusive normative communities. Moreover, there can be norms that require the individual members of a community to treat those of other communities as participants in the same rights as those in which they participate.

To participate in rights-relations with other communities, a community must be able to act as an entity or to authorize action to be taken in its name. Not all communities can do this, and cultural or ethnic minorities that are dispersed through the communities in which they are located may not be able thus to function agentially. Nevertheless, it is possible for articulate and agential subcommunities (sub-subcommunities) to form within such a community. Both the extended community of the Jews and that of American blacks are too widely dispersed to act as communities or authorize their own representation, yet organized subcommunities, articulate and capable of agency, have arisen within both. However, not being authorized representatives of their parent communities, which also encompass other communities with widely varying outlooks, these groups do not speak with their parent communities' voices and cannot act in their names. What they can do is engage in dialogue with other articulate and agential communities or their representatives, including representatives of a state or nation. Such a group may try to secure, from the dominant community, entitlements for its parent community *to be treated as if* it were a participant in institutionalized rights and for this treatment to be extended to their members, individually and collectively. However, entitlements conferred on this basis would be benefits, not rights, affording a weaker protection and establishing a weaker bond of unity and mutual commitment between this subcommunity and the other members of the wider community. This is crucial for the issue of minority rights. I shall try to show that there can and ought to be rights applicable to nonagential communities as such and to their members in virtue of their belonging to those communities, rights that I call 'collective rights'; but this demonstration must be postponed until after discussion of the fundamental rights of individuals and agential communities, on which the argument for collective rights will rest.

GENERIC RIGHTS AND DIALOGIC RECIPROCITY

Human society is distinguished by the compresence and interrelatedness of normative communities of indefinitely many kinds. Every form of communicative social interaction and every social system or organization is an instance of normative community, which is a necessary condition of human existence as we know it. Because it is, whatever conditions are requisite for the existence and continuance of normative community are also necessary conditions of human existence and basic needs of all human beings. Therefore, we have a vital interest in establishing a right to their protection.

This seems paradoxical. If normative communities already exist, why should a right to the conditions of community be necessary? Isn't the assertion that those who are already members of a community are entitled to insurance that the conditions of community will be maintained circular or at best empty? It is no more so than the statement that we must eat in order to (remain alive and) continue to eat. Since normative communities already exist, the conditions that enabled them to form must have obtained. But communities pass out of existence, and the integrity of a community may be threatened, not only by a physical attack but also by an assault on its institutions.[5]

The efficacy of a social norm, its being operative, lies, first, in its being a constituent of the general perspective of a community, internalized by the members as a component of their individual perspectives and, second, in their application of the normative attitude in determining both their own behavior and their expectations regarding one another. A normative community is constituted by its interacting members, who jointly shape and reshape its normative perspective and transmit it to succeeding generations. In this process, the norms are voluntarily adopted. Supposed or intended norms that are merely legislated or are imposed by some individuals or groups upon others are not operative unless and until they are accepted, taken as normative, by those for whom they are to have this weight. This is true not only for the individuals among whom a norm is first instituted, but also for those who are subsequently born into or immigrate into the community, all of whom are expected to apply it to new situations.[6] Transmission of operative norms is their reinstitution, adoption by successive generations who thereby accept their normativity.

Enforced conformity is only a counterfeit of norm-governed behavior. What is accepted in such a case is the authority, not of the norms, but of the enforcing power. To the extent that a government or a dominant subcommunity tries to impose its laws or customs on other subcommunities and their members, the stability of the inclusive community is undermined. A common history and geographic proximity alone are not sufficient conditions of normative community, and the alternative to normative community is *anomie*, alienation, the antithesis of community. If there is to be genuine normative community, the norms must be felt by all to be compelling. For this to be the case, all those who are expected to live by them must participate in their institution, perpetuation, and revision. This means that each must be granted the *authority* to do so: authority to play a part in shaping the community's perspective.

To continue to be operative, norms must be internalized and, when appropriate, applied. However, to apply a norm, to govern oneself by it, is not automatically to do what it calls for, even if one acknowledges its normativity. To apply a normative perspective is to determine one's behavior or judgment in the light of what it defines as relevant and irrelevant, permissible and impermissible, required or optional. Having internalized a particular norm (or norm-complex), we must still, in any situation that elicits it, determine whether and how we will apply it; and factors other than the norm itself—for instance, conflict with other norms—may enter into this determination. The recurrent application of the norms of a community by its members is part of the process by which the norms are not only perpetuated but also either reinforced or modified and efforts to establish new and different norms may be initiated. It is, therefore, an important element in the continuing operation and authority of established norms and the continuity of the general normative perspective of the community. But the need to interpret the norms and decide whether and how to apply them in particular situations is a need to determine the application for ourselves; it is a need for *autonomy*—not total independence but freedom to utilize our own experience and understanding, itself conditioned, although only partly shaped, by the perspectives of the communities to which we belong.

As the condition requisite for social norms—including rights-norms—to become and continue to be operative, the exercise of both authority and autonomy by its members is necessary for the existence of normative community. A true normative community, that is, is a community of self-directing, yet mutually responsive members. Its attainment requires that the exercise of both autonomy and authority be protected, as they can be by institutionalizing them as rights-entitlements in every community, accorded to all and to be respected by all alike. That is, they should be *'generic rights'*. As the conditions of normative community itself, within which all norms and rights are operative, they are the *fundamental* generic rights.

Since communities, in turn, belong to more inclusive communities, the fundamental generic rights should be extended to them. For a community to exercise authority within a wider community is for it to have a voice in the dialogue in which this community of communities not only makes specific decisions but also arrives at principles by which to govern the relations among its members and its relations with other communities. For it to exercise its own authority, speak in its own voice, each subcommunity within the wider community must be free to articulate its own perspective as a community and interpret the norms of the wider community for itself. That is, it must be accepted as an autonomous and authoritative member of the inclusive community and a participant in the self-governance of the whole. The autonomy of a community, in the sense intended here, is not political independence, and granting freedom to the member communities is not a prescription for anarchy. Whether we are talking about the fundamental generic rights of commmunities or of individuals, what is called for is mutual respect for the autonomously exercised authority of all, which necessitates that each participant both submit its (or his or her) judgments and actions to criticism by the others and accept the obligation to be a responsible critic.

A community in which the rights of autonomy and authority are jointly operative, whether it be a community of individuals or a community of communities, is what I call a "community of dialogic reciprocity."[7] To function as such a community is an ideal for which every normative community should strive and in the light of which it ought to be judged. An ideal of unity in diversity, it is the ideal of democracy.

COLLECTIVE RIGHTS

A community that is not able to function in a unified way or engage as a body in communication or interaction with other communities cannot participate in rights-relations as a community. Nevertheless, by the definition of a right, the *members* of such a community, as individuals, ought to participate in all the personal rights operative in the wider community, on an equal basis with all others. No right that is operative in the inclusive community ought to be selectively denied to anyone, which means that no right should be denied on the basis of membership in any subcommunity within it. The fundamental generic rights of every individual to autonomy and authority, especially, should be equally respected by all. But the fact that subcommunities are so often singled out and their members denied what would otherwise be their rights calls for explicit recognition of a second-order generic right, one governing participation in other rights and establishing the entitlement of all the members of every subcommunity to participate in the same rights as those who belong to any other subcommunity. Under the norms governing this right of nondiscriminatory treatment, the obligations as well as the entitlements conferred by all the rights–norms operative in a community would be relevant to all members of each of its subcommunities specifically as members thereof, and applicable to those members collectively. The right of the members of every subcommunity within a state, without exception, to full citizenship is an example.

The right to nondiscriminatory treatment is what I call a collective right. Collective rights, as I am using the term here, are those that are applicable to individuals not simply as such, but on the basis of their collective identity.[8] The ability to participate in these rights is a function, not of any agential powers of their communities, but of those individuals' powers of agency and normative self-governance. Nevertheless, because the members of a community participate in these rights collectively, these rights can also be said to be rights of the communities whose identities they bear. Having such rights entails the members' entitlement *jointly to constitute* a community, a rights-entitlement that can only be a collective one. This is, at the same time, a right of the community they constitute to exist, to be constituted.

The right of collective identity entitles each individual member of every community in which it is operative to share in his or her subcommunity's collective identity without being penalized, to have membership in that community accepted as a legitimate feature of his or her own personal identity, to be accorded the same respect in the wider community as any other collective identity. This right, which like all rights must be mutual, is especially important in view of the role that collective identity plays in the identity and sense of self of every individual. The tendency on the part of many to perceive and feel that people with different ethnic identities are alien can lead them to view these other communities as threats to their personal identity as well as to the identity and existence of their own group. It is this that is at the heart of the suppression of minorities and that makes ethnic conflicts so intractable.[9] And it is this same factor that necessitates mutual respect for all, without exception.

For normative communities, the right of collective identity entails a right of collective autonomy, which entitles the members of a community and the community itself to their own norms and normative practices. An important example is the norms governing linguistic communication within any subcommunity having its own language. The language norms are part of the perspective that identifies such a community and are also part of its members' personal perspectives and ingredient in their collective identity.[10]

It is not immediately clear how there can be a right of collective authority because there would seem to be no way for a nonagential community, even one that has evolved norms, to exercise authority, to participate as a community in interaction or communication with others, or even to authorize a representative to act or speak for it. Nevertheless, nonagential communities can be given a voice in the affairs of a wider community through the use of a poll or referendum to elicit a coherent voice from each.[11] The same mechanism can be employed to enable the members of those subcommunities to select representatives to participate in decision making for the inclusive community. Either procedure can give the subcommunities agential power, at least temporarily, and foster communication and the development of more lasting powers of agency. In short, because we can enable nonagential communities to become articulate, the arguments for the right of authority can also be taken to apply to them. Participation in the establishment of normative principles by those who must abide by them is one of the conditions of the existence of operative norms in the wider community and is, therefore, a condition of the continuing existence and stability of that community itself. This applies to an inclusive community of communities as well as to every segment thereof, and argues for the need to secure the authoritative participation of all subcommunities in the governance of the inclusive community and, hence, for a collective as well as communal right of authority.

ETHNIC CONFLICTS AND THE ROLE OF RIGHTS

Ultimately, the only stable solution to any conflict among communities, including ethnic conflicts, lies in the establishment among the warring parties of an inclusive community of dialogic reciprocity: a community in which each is accepted as an authoritative and autonomous member, equally respected by all as a participant in determining the policies and principles by which the inclusive community is to be governed, both internally and in its relations with yet other communities. It is this ideal of unity-in-multiplicity that I propose as applicable to a multi-ethnic nation. What I am about to suggest is a model of conflict resolution that employs the principle of dialogic reciprocity at two levels: as the goal toward which we need to work and as a means of attaining it.

The first step in conflict resolution must be the establishment of a forum in which all parties to the conflict are represented and each participant understands that the fundamental generic rights are to be extended to all (and to the communities they represent). Only in this way can any of them be assured that their own rights will be respected. For it to be truly representative, the participants in the forum should be democratically elected and responsible to the communities whose authority they bear. It would be desirable if, at each stage, they were to bring the tentative results of their deliberations back to their parent communities for free, open, and critical discussion and a vote or plebiscite to guide them at the next step. This will prolong the deliberations, but it will promote wider acceptance of the result and can help to change the inclusive community or nation into one in which every subcommunity and every member of each is equally empowered to exercise the fundamental rights.

When the affected communities are not geographically centralized or well organized, or when they, too, are torn by internal conflict, it may be difficult even to get them to elect representatives. It may be necessary to start at the local level, asking the diverse groups (sub-subcommunities) in each area or municipality to choose people to participate in the process of electing representatives of their parent subcommunities (in this case, their ethnic communities). By increasing involvement, this program should at the same time strengthen their commitment to the peacemaking process. Granting all the members of every participating group authority as autonomous and responsible partners in this process, with all that this implies, should foster the development of shared perspectives and increase cohesiveness and the sense of community within each (ethnic) community. While the scope of perspectival community may be very limited at first, it should expand even among those who belong to different ethnic communities, since participation in the process will itself provide a common perspective. To say that granting autonomy to all participants is a ground of community might seem contradictory, the autonomy of each being construed as the antithesis of the desired unity. But mutual respect for one another's autonomy and authority entails not only respect for their right to disagree and the right of each to criticize the others, but also the obligation to accept disagreement, to try to understand the perspective from which it emanates, and to make one's own criticisms constructive and take those of others seriously. Acceptance of criticism and disagreement, coupled with respect for every critic and everyone who is the object of criticism, if it can be achieved, will defuse hostility and defensiveness; and attempting to secure the widest possible participation in a dialogue governed by the fundamental rights, while it can prolong deliberations, is time well spent.

Once established, how should a representative body address the practical problems of conflict resolution and the substantive issues around which conflict revolves? The common answer is, "through negotiation." But negotiation is bargaining; it is inherently a struggle for power and results in compromises that almost inevitably cause further discontent. I propose instead an attempt to discover or develop a common perspective, one in which the points at issue appear in a different light from that in which they appear in the perspectives governing the conflict. Such a perspective must be compelling enough to override the perspective of conflict. One that might be efficacious in today's world might be provided by a common interest in economic development, if it could be shown that this can better be achieved through mutual acceptance and trade than by cultivating mutual enmity.[12] Another compelling perspective might be a common need to prevail over external attempts at encroachment or domination.[13] What I am talking about is *the creation and extension of community* rather than an attempt to establish a balance of power. But this can succeed only to the extent that the members and the representatives of each of the conflicting communities believe that their fundamental rights and their integrity as communities will be protected, that their mutual security is not endangered by the dialogue in which they are being asked to engage and will not be so by the agreements at which they arrive. For this to be the case, they must come to understand the nature of rights: that only if all are guaranteed the same rights can the rights of any of them be secured.

When a conflict is so intense and irrational that this process cannot be instituted, the members of a still more inclusive community (such as the United Nations) might decide to employ force to achieve a cessation of hostilities; but such a ceasefire will not hold unless the parties involved can be helped to find a perspective or point of view in terms of which it can be seen as desirable. Given a common perception of even a temporary halt to the conflict as desirable, the rudiments of perspectival community will have been established. This could conceivably pave the way for the contending parties and their representatives to begin to function, at least within a limited context, as participants in a dialogue they understand to be designed to serve them all alike, in the positive outcome of which each has a stake, rather than as rivals for domination. Participation in a common enterprise alone is not guaranteed to stimulate the development of respect for one another's autonomy and authority; but the institution and acceptance of "ground rules," norms governing dialogic interaction, can be a step in this direction, provided these rules are understood by all involved as serving to protect their own autonomy and authority. Acceptance of procedural rules may serve to foster the creation of a new inclusive community in which the existing communities could retain their integrity while yet having reason to respect that of others. Sadly, the nations and peoples of the world provide few models of dialogic reciprocity, but the alternative is perpetual conflict and mutual destruction.

POSTSCRIPT

George Herbert Mead maintained that "If men are capable of recognizing rights as well as of claiming them, then they are capable of forming a community, of establishing institutions whose authority will lie within the community itself."[14] I would amend this to say, "*Only* if men are capable of recognizing rights as well as of claiming them. . . ." Only in legislating to themselves do either individuals or communities bind themselves to obedience; and only when they legislate to themselves and one another jointly is this legislation binding on them all, collectively. Again in Mead's words, "[I]n so far as a member of the community both enacts and obeys the laws of the community a rational state is possible. If laws express the will of the whole community, [the members are] able both to enact them and to obey them. . . . And such laws could express the will of the whole community in so far as they expressed the rights of the members of that community."[15] This is to say that respect for the autonomy and authority of all, without exception—respect for their integrity and their basic rights—is essential if diverse communities are to be united in a single nation.

NOTES

1. See, for example, Loren Lomasky, *Persons, Rights, and the Moral Community* (New York: Oxford University Press, 1987), p. 11, on rights as "the justified claims of individuals against their government and against each other."

2. The legalist tradition, in which rights are viewed as claims against other persons or against society, stems largely from Wesley Newcomb Hohfeld. Cf. his *Fundamental Legal Conceptions*, ed. W. W. Cook (New Haven, Connecticut: Yale University Press, 1919).

3. George Herbert Mead, *Mind, Self, and Society: From the Standpoint of a Social Behaviorist*, ed. Charles W. Morris (Chicago: The University of Chicago Press, 1934), p. 261. Mead's theory is derived in part from

Rousseau's contractarian theory of society, his concept of the "generalized other" being a generalization of the latter's concept of the "general will." Nevertheless, rooted as well in behaviorist psychology and Pragmatism, Mead's view is far different from Rousseau's.

4. Ibid., pp. 163–164, 154.

5. The integrity of a community can also be weakened or destroyed from within by the loss of normative authority. An example of this is when internal conflict causes law and order to break down. Another is when the members of an ethnic community—whether spontaneously or as a result of external pressures—become assimilated into a wider cultural community. In each case a complex of norms that bound the members of a community together, the culture of that community or part of it, has ceased to be operative.

6. It cannot be denied that norms are often applied uncritically and even un–self-consciously. But over the long run, if this happens, norms degenerate into mechanical habits, preserved through the exercise of power rather than acceptance of their prescriptive force.

7. Cf. Chapter 2 above.

8. I also use this term to refer to rights-entitlements that individuals can exercise only collectively, such as language rights.

9. As Terrell A. Northrup points out, "the dynamic of identity . . . plays an important role in the escalation and maintenance of conflict. . . . [T]here are identity-related processes at the individual, social, and structural levels which contribute to intractability, particularly when there are perceived inequities that are construed as a threat to the physical or psychological sense of personal or group self. For both the individual and group who face a threat of invalidation, there is a move to preserve the sense of self. This involves distortion and rigidification, including the tendency to create and enforce separation between parties and the tendency to dehumanize 'enemies.' Through this process, the conflict itself becomes assimilated into the identities of the conflicting parties" ("The Dynamic of Identity in Personal and Social Conflict," in *Intractable Conflicts and Their Transformation*, ed. Louis Kriesberg, Terrell A. Northrup, and Stuart J. Thorson [Syracuse, New York: Syracuse University Press, 1989], p. 76). See also Harold R. Isaacs's *Idols of the Tribe: Group Identity and Political Change* (Cambridge, Massachusetts: Harvard University Press, 1975; repr. 1989), especially Chapters 6–9 on language, history and origins, religion, and nationality.

10. That subcommunities should have a right to their own languages is independent of the question whether their members should be obligated to communicate with others in the common language of the wider community.

11. For its voice to carry weight, the vote of each subcommunity of the inclusive community would have to be taken into account as such; in a vote of this kind, each individual would vote as a member of a subcommunity and then the votes of these communities would be tallied.

12. The interest in economic development is a factor in the move to end hostilities between North and South Korea and between the two Koreas and China. As another example, it has been proposed that the European Community offer membership to all the Balkan states jointly, which, it is suggested, would motivate them to negotiate borders and agreements regarding the treatment of one another's ethnic minorities. An interest, of course, is a kind of perspective. An example (although on a smaller scale) of a perspective dominated by a common interest motivating the resolution of ethnic conflict is provided by an interracial group of mothers, Mothers Against Violence, that formed in Brooklyn, New York, after a 16-year old black youth was set upon and killed by a group of young whites, who were enraged by a report that a white girl had invited some black boys (of whom they thought the victim was one) to a party. The incident was one of a growing number of violent killings of children aged 17 or younger in New York City, a good many of them motivated by ethnic hatred. Edie Bonavita, one of the founders of the group, was quoted in *The New York Times* as saying: "When there is a crisis, when it comes to helping their kids, mothers forget their problems and resentments with other people. They can get the job done" (Felicia R. Lee, "About New York," *The New York Times*, September 12, 1992).

13. Cf. William James, "The Moral Equivalent of War," originally written for and first published by the Association for International Conciliation (Leaflet no. 27); also published in *McClure's Magazine* (August 1910) and *The Popular Science Monthly* (October 1910); in *Essays in Religion and Morality*, The Works of William James, ed. Frederick Burkhardt (Cambridge, Massachusetts: Harvard University Press, 1982), pp. 162–173.

14. George Herbert Mead, *Movements of Thought in the Nineteenth Century*, ed. Merritt H. Moore (Chicago: The University of Chicago Press, 1936), p. 13.

15. Ibid.

5

Difference, Otherness, and the Creation of Community

> Today we are faced with the preeminent fact that, if civilisation is to survive, we must cultivate the science of human relationships—the ability of all people, of all kinds, to live together and work together, in the same world, at peace.
>
> —FRANKLIN DELANO ROOSEVELT[1]

MY PURPOSE HERE is to discuss further the problem of conflict resolution, treating it in terms of the creation of community rather than negotiation or mediation as they are commonly understood and practiced. What I am suggesting is a way of uniting the combatants in a new, inclusive community that will serve them both (or all) and, at the same time, preserve the integrity of each. To locate the discussion in a theoretical context, I shall review some points about the concept of community and several related concepts.

THE CONCEPT OF COMMUNITY

When its meaning is not simply taken for granted, the term 'community' is often used by philosophers in narrow senses, as when Josiah Royce maintains that a true community is not only one that has a history and established institutions, but also one whose members are conscious of their common history.[2] This rules out many kinds of community, including linguistic communities. Royce's use of the term is an honorific one, as is John Dewey's in those contexts in which he identifies community and democracy.[3] Acknowledging that the word 'community' is used in a number of different senses, the contemporary writer R. E. Ewin states that he is using it to refer to "a group of people who can act and speak as one . . . such that we sensibly speak of what the group decided or what the group did."[4] That is, he limits the concept to what I call "agential" communities, a category that would include a mob as well as a committee or a citizenry empowered with the vote but would exclude communities such as the academic community, which is too widely dispersed to act as a unit.

What we need is a value-neutral sense of this term that is broad enough to encompass communities of all kinds. In the generic sense provided by Justus Buchler, persons are joined in community by sharing an attitude or perspective. As Buchler puts it, "what makes the being of any community is not so much the homogeneity of individuals as the potency for many individuals of a given natural complex."[5] An example of community in this sense is the community of those who appreciate beauty. Its existence does not presuppose interaction among its members or conscious identification with it, or awareness of its history—or that it have a history. Such a community, which I call a "perspectival community," may even be "invisible," its existence unnoted. The main importance of perspectival community is that sharing a perspective is the indispensable precondition of communication and mutual understanding. (This is the case, despite the fact that, by their content, some perspectives militate against particular actualizations of this potentiality.)

As I have noted in earlier chapters, George Herbert Mead defines community in terms not merely of shared perspective, but of the kind of perspective he calls "the attitude of a generalized other." By this he means an organized set of understandings and expectations that govern what he calls "institutions": established ways of acting and responding, including the use of gestures and symbols and the organized behavior patterns that constitute social roles.[6] Whereas sharing a perspective in Buchler's generic sense is a necessary condition of communication and meaningful social interaction, sharing the attitude or perspective of a generalized other is the sufficient condition. In my own terminology, persons who share a normative perspective constitute a "normative community." All speakers of Russian constitute such a community; so do performers and their audiences, who understand their respective roles in terms of a commonly understood set of norms.

Every individual human being belongs to indefinitely many

communities, both perspectival and normative. Each one's personal perspective is complex and intersects with those of many others. Analogously, communities and their perspectives intersect in innumerable ways, and a given community may encompass indefinitely many subcommunities. Moreover, there are different kinds of community. There are face-to-face communities and communities whose members may never come to know or interact with one another, communities that are organized and those (like that of English speakers) that are not. Some communities are long-lasting and others transient; some, but not all, are capable of acting as entities. Some are self-conscious, in the sense that those who belong to them recognize themselves and one another as doing so, whereas others (like the perspectival community of those who fear heights or the normative community of dictionary users) are not. The most highly self-conscious communities are those that sociologists call "reference groups": communities whose members identify with one another and with whose interests they see their own to be bound up.[7] But while each of us may identify most strongly with a primary reference group—often an ethnic group, sometimes a religious one—the perspective of even that community is only one constituent of our personal perspective as an individual self. A community is not a collection of persons with identical outlooks or behavior patterns. The condition of community is one of sameness-in-difference, of partial commonality of perspective among persons whose perspectives as individuals also include other perspectives, some unique to themselves and some shared with members of the multiple communities to which they also belong: families, occupational communities, friendship groups, religious communities, political movements, and so forth.

CULTURE AND COMMUNITY; DIFFERENCE AND OTHERNESS

The word 'culture' is also used in several ways in connection with human communities. We speak of "the culture of science" as well as the "cultures" of different peoples or ethnic communities, and we sometimes refer to a people as a culture. The culture of an ethnic community is a system of norms or institutions comprehensive enough to constitute a way of life. A cultural community in this sense is a self-conscious one, and for its members—at least those born into it—is likely to be an important reference group, essential to their sense of identity as well as a source of their characteristic ways of behaving and viewing the world. Nevertheless, individual differences and differences among subgroups in the community retain their significance.

Members of a self-conscious community are inevitably aware of differences between their community and other communities, and between themselves and the members of those other communities. But recognizing that persons, whether individually or collectively, are different from oneself is not necessarily to view them as alien, or as better or worse than oneself, and it need not be a hostile attitude or one accompanied by fear. An American is likely to find aspects of Japanese comportment not only different, but puzzling; yet despite the history of war between our countries, Americans who encounter them today typically accept the Japanese and their culture. In the perspective of these Americans, difference is recognized but neither disdained nor feared. However, there is a second perspective that we might call one of "otherness" that involves a sense of social distance based on a negative and sometimes hostile response and a feeling that the other is, somehow, a threat to oneself or to a community with which one identifies.[8] Such an attitude toward one or more groups of outsiders may come to be an important element in the perspective of a given community or of a significant subcommunity within it. A strong sense of otherness, especially when it is mutual, may feed or even generate conflict among communities, and it can be deliberately fostered, as can the conflicts to which, in turn, it lends support. But it may also arise as a consequence of conflicts that stem from other sources (such as conflicts over territory). The perspective of difference, in contrast, permits acceptance and tolerance, and allows those who hold it to value diversity as well as to like and even admire traits that differ from their own.

Conflicts are not always based on perceived differences. Communities, like individuals who view one another as competitors, may fight one another precisely because of perceived similarities among them, each motivated by a concern for its own interests, which, because of their parallelism, they take to be incompatible with the others'. The sense of otherness here rests on presumed similarity, not difference. But the perspective of otherness is most visible and most powerful today in the ethnic and tribal conflicts of the sort we are seeing in so many places. And, whether open or incipient, the conflicts among ethnic communities in the United States express the same attitude. While they may reflect real socioeconomic grievances, these conflicts are increasingly motivated by hatred of the other *as* other, the attitude of the combatants characterized by prejudice toward and fear of the culture and the person of the other, individually and collectively. Here, as elsewhere, the sense of otherness is sometimes deliberately cultivated in order to sharpen the hostility of the participants. To some extent, the perspective of otherness is a feature of every social conflict, but in what follows, I shall primarily have in mind conflicts in which it is dominant, particularly those among ethnic communities.

COMMUNITY AND CONFLICT

The methods customarily employed in attempts to resolve conflict are negotiation and mediation. That negotiations so often fail is because neither party wishes to give up what it has been fighting for. Any settlement that is achieved is likely to be a compromise, sowing the seed of further conflict. Mediation, on the other hand, usually consists in the mediator's proposing a solution designed to be as unobjectionable as possible to all parties to the conflict, who then negotiate with the mediator to secure terms that they deem more appropriate or that they see to be more favorable to themselves. Even if it is successful in alleviating the conflict at hand, mediation of this sort may leave a residue of dissatisfaction similar to that which can remain as an outcome of any other negotiation. Ideally, the way to resolve a conflict would be to alter the conditions that engendered it, but this is seldom possible, and those conditions too often include the attitudes of the combatants toward one another. Alternatively, we might devise a new way of looking at the situation, one that places it in a different light and compels a more constructive response. Part of what this new perspective must accomplish is to help bring about a change in the attitudes of the opposing parties toward one another, to help them overcome their hostility and fear and the pervasive attitude of otherness. At the same time, if it is not to pose a threat to the parties involved, it is important not to jeopardize their sense of their own identity or their freedom to participate in determining their future. To this end, whatever steps we take must foster the mutual acceptance of difference.

To suggest the development of a perspective to be shared by those who have been engaged in conflict is to suggest the creation of a new, inclusive perspectival community, opening the way for fresh communication and interaction. But this alone is not guaranteed to alleviate hostility or put an end to conflict. The members of a community do not necessarily interact or, if they do, relate positively or constructively to one another. To the extent that they respond to one another in ways that are mutually intelligible, the parties to a conflict actually constitute a community already: They are engaged in communicative interaction, responding to one another in ways that are mutually intelligible. (This is not to deny that hostility toward others, even when it is mutual, can sometimes be blind and uncomprehending.) Depending on its content and its form, communication may exacerbate existing hostility or even serve to create hostility. Through misunderstanding if not by design, it can reinforce the estrangement between the parties to a conflict. And even where there is not open combat, people may share a perspective that is potentially one of conflict, an attitude of mutual resentment, say, or mistrust.

Nevertheless, community and communication are essential to peaceful interaction, and even communities that are hostile to one another may share perspectives that, whether or not they are aware of them, join them in an inclusive community that is potentially one of mutual support and cooperation. Building on William James's call for "a moral equivalent of war"—which James looked to as a way of producing social cohesion among people who had been but are no longer united against a common enemy—Mead sought, in his paper "National-Mindedness and International-Mindedness," a way to ensure a lasting peace in the aftermath of World War II.[9] "The moral equivalent of war," he wrote, "is found in the intelligence and the will both to discover

. . . common interests between contending nations and to make them the basis for the solution of the existing differences and for the common life which they will make possible" (NM 366). That is, discovery of common interests can serve to unite people in a self-conscious community. Where "common goods do become the ends of the individuals of the community," Mead says, they develop "solidarity": a "sense of common selfhood" (NM 369). But if this is to endure, he insists, joining in community with other nations must not entail the sacrifice of national cohesion and national pride.

Adopting Mead's approach, we would endeavor to resolve conflicts by seeking some common interest or goal that is important enough to induce the conflicting parties to settle their differences and work together for a common end. That is, we would try to identify a community of interest—a perspectival community—on which to build an active and agential normative community. Supposing the conflict to be that among the ethnic communities in Flint, Michigan, for example, we might try to build an effective, inclusive community around the common need to rebuild the city's shattered economy. But how should this community operate? What can secure the continuing cooperation of former antagonists? What will prevent the members of each group from feeling that their own collective identity is threatened by a process to which it might seem they have subordinated their independence? How can they foster appreciation of difference and help decrease the sense of otherness?

We can look for help to Dewey's concept of the method of democracy, the experimental method of organized intelligence, and to Mead's ideal of universality and mutuality. Both are designed to preserve diversity within the framework of community, and, as far as possible, to serve the separate interests of the participants together with those interests they share. The problem in conflict resolution, Dewey says, "is precisely *how* conflicting claims are to be settled in the interest of the widest possible contribution to the interests of all—or at least of the great majority."[10] He proposes "to bring these conflicts out into the open where their special claims can be seen and appraised, where they can be discussed and judged in the light of more inclusive interests than are represented by either of them separately" (LSA 56). And, in another context, he calls for a democratic political process in which "all those who are affected by social institutions . . . have a share in producing and managing them."[11]

Rather than simply the rule of the majority, Dewey sees the method of democracy to be a cooperative exercise of the pragmatist method of problem-solving, a method of inquiry akin to the method of science. It is experimental in that it involves open discussion and critical evaluation at every step of the way, even of its own procedures. Stressing a different aspect, Mead identifies the ideal of democracy with the attitude of universal brotherhood he finds embodied in "the universal religions," an attitude that holds every individual "to stand on the same level with every other" (MSS 286). Politically, he finds the same egalitarian principle in Jean-Jacques Rousseau's *Social Contract*, in the idea of a society "in which the individual maintains himself as a citizen only to the degree that he recognizes the rights of everyone else to belong to the same community" (MSS 286). Whether among individuals or among communities, Mead sees the democratic ideal as one of mutual self-realization through functional differentiation, similar to what he finds in economic life, where difference is valued and respected precisely because it serves a common interest. In a democratic society, "the individual realizes himself in others through that which he does as peculiar to himself" (MSS 289). In a democratic international community, which he takes the League of Nations to be, "[t]he smallest community is in a position to express itself just because it recognizes the right of every other nation to do the same." It would follow, to paraphrase Mead, that, in any truly democratic community, every subcommunity recognizes every other subcommunity in the very process of asserting itself (cf. MSS 287).

At the heart of Mead's religious and political conception of democracy is the idea that it is potentially universal. Given the centrality of communication in his thought, it should not surprise us that he takes as the model of universal community that of a universal community of discourse, epitomized by logical discourse. Here, every participant uses the same terms and understands them in the same way, so that, whether communicating his or her own intent or interpreting the communications of others, each one is taking the same attitude. "If communication can be carried through and made perfect," Mead says, "then there would exist the kind of democracy to which we have referred, in which each individual would carry just the response in himself that he knows he calls out in the community" (MSS 327). But commonality or universality of response, mutual understanding, does not preclude individuality. While responding as a member of this community we remain ourselves, our identity partly determined by the other communities to which we belong.

OVERCOMING OTHERNESS

Extrapolating from what I have said, I would like to outline a strategy for overcoming otherness and reconciling communities that have come into conflict with one another. While I have in mind conflicts among ethnic communities, I believe the proposal is applicable to conflicts of other sorts as well. The procedure I suggest would incorporate the following three steps:

(1) Identify a compelling need, goal, or interest that is common to as many members of the opposing communities as possible, or a problem that they all share and whose solution would be in the interest of all. If they are not aware of any such interest, it may be necessary to point one out to them and show them how they might be served if it could be satisfied. What I am proposing, in other words, is to search for or cultivate an attitude that joins the members of the conflicting communities in a wider community of interest—a kind of perspectival community—and to help them not only to recognize that they have this interest in common but to feel comfortable with this fact. Important to this enterprise is that the interest defined by the shared attitude be one that can best be served by means of a joint effort. Examples might be a common need to stop or prevent an epidemic (AIDS, for instance), the need to improve the quality of the common water supply, or a desire to improve public transportation in a region both groups inhabit.

(2) The next step would be to develop this perspectival community into a community of inquiry: a normative community dedicated to cooperative and exploratory ("experimental") discourse regarding the way in which the common goal can best be

understood and the means by which it might be reached. Among the norms of this community, as of an ideal scientific community, should be the principle that all discussion be open and public, and that the contributions and the viewpoints of all participants be taken equally seriously and equally carefully and critically considered. The latter is the principle I have called "dialogic reciprocity."[12] In a process designed to help in the resolution of intergroup conflict, another normative principle ought to be that, as far as possible, where the needs of the participants differ, these too should be taken into consideration in determining how best to further the interest in which they all share. Participation in joint inquiry under these conditions should help to replace the sense of "otherness" with acceptance of and, it is to be hoped, mutual respect for one another. It might serve as well to cultivate an acceptance of differences in other areas: in the present context, the cultural differences that had been the focus of mutual alienation and hostility.

(3) Finally, as Dewey recommends, the process of inquiry itself would need to be carefully structured and conscientiously monitored. The participants (the members of the contending communities, working if necessary through their chosen representatives) should establish rules of procedure that all understand and accept, as well as a common vocabulary of carefully defined terms. As they proceed, they should keep both under review, revising them when necessary in order to ensure clarity and mutual intelligibility and avoid misunderstanding. This, in turn, should serve to strengthen the bonds of community among the participants in the inquiry and facilitate the extension of this community to other areas of concern.

NOTES

1. From a speech that was to be given the day after Roosevelt died. Reported in *The Guardian Weekly*, Volume 156, Issue 12 (for the week ending March 23, 1997).

2. Josiah Royce, *The Problem of Christianity* II (New York: The Macmillan Co., 1913), Lecture IX.

3. For example, "The clear consciousness of a communal life, in all

of its implications, constitutes the idea of democracy." *The Public and Its Problems* (1927), in *John Dewey: The Later Works*. II. *1925–1927*, ed. Jo Ann Boydston (Carbondale and Edwardsville: Southern Illinois University Press, 1988), p. 328. Cf. Beth J. Singer, "Dewey's Concept of Community: A Critique," *Journal of the History of Philosophy*, 23, No. 4 (October 1985), 555–569.

4. R. E. Ewin, *Liberty, Community, and Justice* (Totowa, New Jersey: Rowman & Littlefield, 1987), p. 7. Ewin's view is also honorific. "At the foundations of communal life," he maintains, "people must treat on the basis of equality" (p. 39). On this assumption, a society or state in which there is an established status hierarchy would not be a community.

5. Justus Buchler, *Toward a General Theory of Human Judgment* (New York: Columbia University Press, 1951), p. 40.

6. George Herbert Mead, *Mind, Self, and Society: From the Standpoint of a Social Behaviorist*, ed. Charles W. Morris (Chicago: The University of Chicago Press, 1934), pp. 211, 260–262; hereafter cited as MSS.

7. Cf. Robert K. Merton, "Contributions to the Theory of Reference Group Behavior," in *Continuities in Social Research: Studies in the Scope and Method of the American Soldier*, ed. Robert K. Merton and Paul F. Lazarsfeld (Glencoe, Illinois: The Free Press, 1950), pp. 40–105.

8. Cf. Zillah Eisenstein, *Hatreds: Racialized and Sexualized Conflicts in the Twenty-First Century* (New York: Routledge, 1996), p.13.

9. William James, "The Moral Equivalent of War," in *Essays in Religion and Morality*, The Works of William James, ed. Frederick Burkhardt (Cambridge, Massachusetts: Harvard University Press, 1982), pp. 162–173; George Herbert Mead, "National-Mindedness and International Mindedness," *International Journal of Ethics*, 39 (1929), 392–407, repr. in George Herbert Mead, *Selected Writings*, ed. Andrew J. Reck (Indianapolis, New York, and Kansas City: Bobbs-Merrill, 1964), pp. 355–370; hereafter cited as NM.

10. John Dewey, *Liberalism and Social Action* (1935), in *John Dewey: The Later Works*. XI. *1935–1937*, ed. Jo Ann Boydston (Carbondale and Edwardsville: Southern Illinois University Press, 1991), p. 56. Hereafter cited as LSA.

11. Dewey, "Democracy and Educational Administration," *Official Report of the Convention of the Department of Superintendence of the National Education Association* (Washington, D.C.: American Association of School Administrators, March 1937), pp. 48–55; repr. in *John Dewey: The Later Works*. XI. *1935–1937*, ed. Jo Ann Boydston (Carbondale and Edwardsville: Southern Illinois University Press, 1991), pp. 217–218.

12. See chapter 2 above.

6

Multiculturalism, Identity, and Minority Rights: Will Kymlicka and the Concept of Special Rights

DESPITE THE CLOSE LINKS between culture and geography, the result of centuries of history is that most of the countries or political states in the world today are multicultural, including within their boundaries the inheritors of more than one cultural tradition. Whether these boundaries are the result of war and conquest, of treaties entered into for economic, political, or religious reasons, or are the heritage of colonial occupation, such countries vary in the degree of stability they have attained, and, at the present time, ethnic strife is rampant all over the globe. Added to this is the factor of prejudice against immigrant groups. In the interest of peace and equality, it would be preferable if people would recognize their common humanity rather than dwell on the differences that divide them. This sentiment is eloquently expressed in a video produced by a group of antinationalists in Sarajevo, whose message to the world is a cry from the heart: "There are no Bosnians, Croats, or Serbs! There are only citizens!"[1] But what distinguishes human society from that of other social species is precisely that human behavior and relations are shaped not merely by culture, but also by a multiplicity of different cultures; and even though different cultures share common features, and communication among them is possible, it is not likely that cultural differences can ever be obliterated.

Moreover, cultural minorities worldwide are clamoring for legal protection and implementation of the right of self-determination that is guaranteed to them by the International Covenants on Economic, Social, and Cultural Rights and on Civil and Political Rights. On the practical side, this raises a question as to how cultural pluralism can be encouraged without increasing the danger of conflict. The question has also been raised as to whether the universalist principles regarding human rights, embodied in such documents as the U.S. Bill of Rights, the Canadian Charter, and the Universal Declaration of Human Rights, are compatible with legislation designed to preserve ethnic pluralism (since not every culture respects all the rights specified therein). In addition, there is an inconsistency within General Assembly Resolution 1514. Article I states that "all peoples have the right to self-determination. By virtue of that right they freely determine their political status and freely pursue their economic, social and cultural development." Freedom to determine their political status would have to include freedom to opt for independence; but paragraph 6 of the Resolution specifies that "[a]ny attempt at the partial or total disruption of the national unity and territorial integrity of the country is incompatible with the purposes and principles of the Charter of the United Nations."

In this chapter I shall not be concerned with political independence. I shall focus instead on the arguments of the Canadian philosopher Will Kymlicka for "special rights" designed to protect indigenous minorities and their cultures.[2] As Kymlicka points out, countries may be multicultural in more than one sense. In his terminology, they may be multinational or multiethnic or may combine the two.[3] That is, in addition to peoples whose homelands (whether by origin or conquest or as a result of mass migration in the past) lie within the territory of a sovereign state, such a state may encompass immigrants and their descendants who have made a life for themselves away from their native lands. Immigrants, however, and the generations that succeed them, may still identify themselves and one another in terms of their cultural and historical background; they may cling to their native tongues, their religions, and, interestingly enough, their cuisines. In common as well as scholarly English usage, this cultural and historical identity is often referred to as 'nationality'. This term is confusing, however, because 'nation' is used in English as a synonym for 'country' or 'nation-state', and 'nationality' commonly has the same connotation. To make the distinction clear, Kymlicka uses the term 'ethnicity' rather than 'nationality' to refer to the cultural identity of immigrants. Nevertheless, as when he distinguishes between multiethnic and multinational countries, he speaks of indigenous peoples as "nations." To avoid ambiguity in what follows, I shall not do this, but normally use his alternate terms, 'peoples' or 'indigenous peoples'. For immigrant groups, I shall use the term 'ethnic group'. However, when the distinction between them is not important, I shall speak of both as 'cultural communities'. I shall try to avoid the term 'nation'. The term 'state' is also used ambiguously to refer to an independent country or nation-state and to a government, but the ambiguity is avoided if we distinguish between *a* state (country) and *the* state (government).

Either a people or an immigrant group may be a minority (or the majority) within a country or state; but even when it is a minority, unless it is destroyed militarily or by economic or political forces, a people, with ties to a geographic location, is more likely to retain its cultural integrity and cohesiveness. When individuals or families emigrate and settle in countries with languages and customs different from their own and with different social, political, and economic institutions to which they must adapt in order to survive, especially if they are geographically separated from one another, it is difficult for them to maintain many of their traditional institutions, and the members of successive generations may not even wish to. To the extent that they assimilate and lose their distinctive cultural traits, their sense of communal identity may weaken, although, especially in the case of minorities defending themselves against a dominant and more powerful majority, assimilation may be resisted and the sense of cultural identity deliberately reinforced. We see this, for instance, in some of the Chinese, Jewish, and Greek communities in American cities. In New York City, there are annual celebrations of Italian, Haitian, Jamaican, Puerto Rican, and other minority identities, and schools where children are taught their Chinese or Greek or other minority languages and cultural practices. But even when individuals have assimilated, the members of other cultural communities are still likely to single them out, to categorize them in terms of their respective ethnic and geographic backgrounds and their place in the political and economic hierarchy. Conspicuously, each cultural group is apt to look down upon at least some of the "others."

I have been distinguishing between majority and minority communities, but the terms 'majority' and 'minority' are not always used to refer to numerical proportions. Instead, a cultural group that is politically and economically dominant will usually be identified as the majority, and those that are subordinate will be classed as minorities. As Jay Sigler has said, "In its simplest form we can regard as a minority any group [or] category of people who can be identified by a sizable segment of the population as objects for prejudice or discrimination or who, for reasons of deprivation, require the positive assistance of the state. A persistent nondominant position of the group in political, social, and cultural matters is the common feature of the minority."[4] Social stratification can be complex, involving socioeconomic class, sex, or physical characteristics (actual or imputed) as well as culture traits; the "majority–minority" distinction is used to mark as higher or lower on the social scale communities identifiable either by appearance—so-called "racial" characteristics—or by culture traits, or by a combination of the two. "Racial" characteristics such as color, hair color and texture, height, facial structure or eye shape occurring along a broad continuum, it is possible for those at the "correct" end of such a continuum to "pass" as members of the privileged majority, provided they are sufficiently acculturated. In any case, the assignment of racial identity, whether to individuals or to peoples, is often arbitrary. An article in *The New York Times*, for instance, reported from Rwanda that a Hutu physician was able to save the life of a teenage Tutsi boy by claiming him as his son. Despite the fact that the distinction is based on physical characteristics, the Hutu guards at a checkpoint could not tell from his appearance that the boy was not a Hutu. And, as Lawrence Wright has noted regarding the United States, "At times, we have counted as 'races' different national groups [i.e., citizens of other political states], such as Mexicans and Filipinos. Some Asian Indians were counted as members of a 'Hindu' race in the censuses from 1920 to 1940; then they became white for three decades."[5] Nevertheless, race is very often taken to be a component—sometimes the key component—of cultural identity or ethnicity.

I shall be concerned here with the problem of how we should treat cultural communities that have minority status and whose members are trying to preserve their traditions and their communal integrity. Many such communities satisfy the requirements of what Kymlicka would call "nations," but some, such as the Jews (who constitute a diversified and scattered, but nevertheless identifiable, cultural community) or the Mexican-Americans in the United States, do not. On the basis of the theory of rights that I have advanced, I have argued that all cultural communities should have a right to exist and that the members of every such community should have the collective right to preserve their culture. (As I have argued, this does not entail permitting communities to deprive other such communities or any of their own members of rights.) In the terminology I have used, for them to have this right means that both the communities as such, and their members, individually and collectively, should have the rights of autonomy and authority. (By 'autonomy' as applied to a community, it should be remembered, I mean practical and cultural self-determination rather than political independence.) I shall focus the discussion on Kymlicka's proposal for granting special status to indigenous peoples and the grounds on which he justifies it. While it was developed explicitly with reference to legislation regarding indigenous peoples in Canada, aspects of Kymlicka's plan could be more widely applicable. At the same time, I find that his proposal and the analysis on which it rests present a number of problems, and discussion of these may shed light on the more general issues.

I

The contention that cultural communities ought to be preserved or protected raises a question regarding their significance and moral status. Beginning with the social contract theorists Hobbes and Locke, most modern Western philosophers have taken an individualist position, asserting the ontological and moral primacy of the individual and giving the communities to which the individual belongs only derivative status and value. Neo-Kantians, too, adopt a strong individualist stance, taking the moral value of the individual to rest on the fact of moral autonomy, on what they take to be an innate human ability to prescribe valid, universal moral principles and to understand that one ought to follow them. Thus, the human individual, and only the human individual, has intrinsic value. More recently, under the influence of Hegel, the concept of man as an inherently social animal, found in both Aristotle and Mill, has been given a new interpretation, with important implications for the concept of moral judgment as well as the understanding of the relative ontological and moral status of individual and community.

Philosophers of the communitarian school maintain, in opposition to Kant, that moral judgment is necessarily conditioned and shaped by cultural traditions (Hegel's *Sittlichkeit*), and that the self that makes moral judgments is no independent, individual existent but constituted *as* a self by the cultural community to which it belongs. A community, on this view, is a unity, not a collection of independent individuals; individuals are what they are only as members of communities, so that the individual cannot be ontologically or psychologically prior to the community. Membership in a community is a necessary condition of selfhood; and culture, being the precondition of moral judgment, is the source of the individual's moral autonomy. Hence, communitarians assign intrinsic value to cultural communities and to membership in them. It would thus seem natural for them to defend the principle that cultural communities should be preserved. On the other hand, just as they see individual rights to be a threat to the welfare of a community (I shall discuss this idea in Chapter 9), some communitarians might find the existence and cultural autonomy of subcommunities within a more inclusive community such as a political state to be a threat to the integrity of the latter.

Individualists, in contrast (fashionably identified these days as "liberals"), may question the very existence of communities on the ground that they are "superpersonal entities"; or they may hold communal autonomy, if it is in some way possible, to conflict with the autonomy or the rights of the community's individual members. Still, not all who take the individualist position that communities or groups are nothing over and above their members deny the possibility or legitimacy of group autonomy. Larry May, for instance (as I have noted), holds that "[g]roups do not exist in their own right," and reduces them, not to individuals as such, but to "individuals in relationships." But he goes on to take the "pragmatic" position that "if a collection of persons displays the ability to engage in joint action or to have common interests, then this collection of persons should be conceived as a group." He contends, moreover, that even though the critical reflection essential to autonomy can only be "carried out *vicariously* by any group through, and by means of, the critical and creative reflections of its individual members . . . it makes sense to understand human groups of all kinds . . . as having the potential for a kind of autonomy expressing itself in the way they carry out their joint ventures, and hence as having a collective autonomy." And, while he defends individual rights, he argues as well that "the understanding of such concepts as 'responsibility', 'rights', and 'justice' should be adjusted to fit cases which do not involve merely isolated individual actors and actions."[6]

In his *Liberalism, Community, and Culture*, Will Kymlicka strongly defends the proposition that indigenous peoples ought to be protected and advocates that they be given special rights, but he does so on individualist grounds.[7] Kymlicka is primarily interested in defending liberalism, but he reformulates the liberal position so as to accommodate his own: "Liberalism, as I've presented it, is characterized both by a certain kind of individualism—that is, individuals are viewed as the ultimate units of moral worth, as having moral standing as ends in themselves, . . . and by a certain kind of *egalitarianism*—that is, every individual has an equal moral status, and hence is to be treated as an equal by the government, with equal concern and respect" (LCC 140). In the history of Western ethical and political thought, as I have indicated, this moral or ethical individualism and egalitarianism rest on a metaphysical or ontological individualism, an atomistic view that takes individual persons to be independent, unitary existents. While he does not abandon the individualist ethic, Kymlicka modifies the metaphysical individualism with which it is associated to take into account the fact that membership in a cultural community is a constituent of an individual person's identity. But I believe he fails to substantiate his claim regarding the relation between communal membership and personal identity, partly because of an ambiguity in his use of the term 'identity' and partly because he lacks

a sufficiently precise (metaphysical) analysis of what personal
identity is.

Kymlicka rests his argument for the rights of cultural minorities
on the fact that membership in a cultural community is "an important good for the individual." He finds this good to be, in the
first place, a function of the relation between membership in cultural communities and personal identity: "People are bound, in
an important way, to their own cultural community. We can't just
transplant people from one culture to another, even if we provide
the opportunity to learn the other language and culture. Someone's upbringing isn't something that can just be erased; it is, and
will remain, a constitutive part of who that person is" (LCC 175).
The expression "constitutive part of who that person is" here
seems to imply that the community in some way actually contributes to the character and personality of the individual brought
up in it. What Kymlicka stresses, however, is not so much identity
as such, the traits that distinguish a person as a particular, identifiable self, as the *sense* of identity (the sense of being who one is, as
an individual and as a member of one's community). His point is
that "[c]ultural membership affects *our very sense of personal identity
and capacity*," and he speaks of a person's "cultural heritage" as
"the sense of belonging to a cultural structure and history" (LCC
175; emphasis added). This shift results in his overlooking the role
of culture and, within it, the special role of language, in shaping
the broad outlines of individual selfhood: their "constitutive" role
(to use Kymlicka's own term) in determining "who a person is."
He seems to be thinking of identity more as a matter of "identify-
ing with" than as consisting in the traits by which a person can be
identif*ied*, recognized. The latter would include, in addition to
such traits as that person's appearance and voice, the characteristic
ways in which she or he deals with the world and with other
people. Identity in this sense can include having a sense of belonging to a cultural community (as well as to other communities); that one identifies with one's cultural community, if one
does so, is a personal trait. But this says little about the role of
culture in relation to the other aspects of one's character and personality.

Kymlicka's main argument for the value of cultural membership, however, for its being "an important good" for the individ-

ual, is that "the cultural structure [provides] a context of choice" (LCC 166). "[M]y proposal claims that cultural community enters our self-understandings by providing a context of choice within which to choose and pursue our conception of the good life" (LCC 172). He goes on to say, "The primary good being recognized is the cultural *community* as a context of choice, not the character of the community or its traditional ways of life, which people are free to endorse or reject" (LCC 172; emphasis added).

Kymlicka points out that there are two senses in which the term 'culture' is used: it refers to "the *character* of a historical community" and also to "the cultural community or structure itself" (LCC 167). Arguing that a cultural community "continues to exist even when its members are free to modify the character of the culture" (and presumably even when they actually do so), he uses the term 'culture' almost exclusively in the second sense, to refer to a community of persons (LCC 167). Linguistic usage aside, I agree that there is a distinction to be made between cultural communities and their culture patterns (their "character" or "way of life"); I also agree that cultural communities persist even when their cultures change; and I emphatically agree that cultural norms are and should be open to criticism and that the members of any community should be free to modify its culture. But I believe it is Kymlicka who confuses the community with its culture, and I think this is because he has no precise definition of the latter. I believe it is this lack that is responsible both for his failure to distinguish between identity and the sense of identity and for an important confusion in his concept of a "context of choice."

To say that the cultural community to which we belong "enters our *self-understandings*" echoes the notion of cultural membership affecting our *sense of* personal identity and capacity. Neither is false, but, in addition, the culture of this community enters into the constitution of our selves, our identifiable character and the capacities that we develop, and, as I shall show, one of the ways in which it does so is by providing contexts of choice.

According to Kymlicka, the context of choice is that which "provid[es] meaningful options for us" (LCC 166). But what functions in this way is the framework of beliefs, understandings, and attitudes in terms of which we judge the situations in which we find ourselves. It is the perspective in which we view a situation that leads us to understand both that it affords us options and what those options are. This framework is not an instantaneous development; nor is it a purely individual construct. In its outlines, it derives from the culture of our community: habitual attitudes and understandings that are operative in the community and are social norms. Such attitudes and understandings structure our personal perspectives, conditioning (though not fully determining) the way we perceive and interpret the things, the people, the situations that we encounter. This, however, is not what Kymlicka intends. By "context" here, he makes clear that he means *social* context, in the sense of the community of persons within which the chooser is located and with which she or he identifies—the reference group—not the culture of that community (its "character" or "traditional way of life").[8] But as that which provides meaningful options—which determines our understanding of the options open to us—the social context within which choices are made, the community is not separable from *the attitudinal and cognitive context provided by its culture.* It is social norms that provide a "context of choice" in the latter sense, by structuring the way we perceive a situation, our interpretation of it as a situation of choice; and they delineate a range of alternatives available to or conceivable by the chooser. Given this framework, the chooser can apply *additional* perspectives, and even devise *new*, original perspectives, that modify his or her understanding of the situation, before ultimately arriving at a choice. But the choice is culturally conditioned: any choice that is not will be viewed as inappropriate, wrong-headed, or "off the wall" by other members of the community.

The community of persons to which we belong and with which we identify does indeed provide us with this attitudinal and cognitive context by imbuing us with its culture; but the two are not the same. Again, conscious identification with the community may contribute significantly to our sense of who we are, and recognition that our judgments are consonant with those of the people with whom we identify may strengthen our confidence in our choices, give us "the courage of our convictions"; but it is the *perspective* of the community that frames our choices, and it does so because it has helped to mold us as choosers. Insofar as we have internalized its norms—insofar as we have become

acculturated—the community shapes our attitudes and understandings, our beliefs and our values, our expectations and our
dispositions to act. The ethnic or cultural community to which
we belong, which plays such a large role in our experience, is not
the only community that functions in this way. Each of us belongs
to many communities that have their own normative perspectives, and some of those perspectives, those of religious and occupational communities among them, may be transcultural. Each of
these perspectives defines parameters of choice, a range of ends,
means, and long-term goals that are open to us. Moreover, all the
perspectives that we acquire enter into our character and identity
as selves. But the perspective of our cultural community, instilled
in us through our "upbringing," makes the most important and
lasting contribution to our personal identity—to who we are.
And even though it changes as time goes on, it is this perspective,
transmitted from generation to generation, that constitutes "the
character of the community," stable in some respects, changing
in others, but expressed in its distinctive institutions and "its traditional ways of life."

Culture in the broadest (generic) sense, the sense in which we
can speak of the culture of science or the culture of the "beat
generation," is the attitude of any generalized other. The kind of
culture at issue here, ethnic culture, is that of a community of
persons with a common geographic origin and a common history;
a community that has, during that history, evolved a comprehensive way of life—language, customs, beliefs, practices, arts. A cultural community is a self-conscious community. We identify
ourselves as members of our cultural community and feel kinship
with other members. We expect them to understand us, and we
take into consideration what we think would be their response to
what we say or do. But without the shared perspectival framework that unites us with them in mutual understanding, we and
they would not constitute a community in the first place, and
their responses would be both unpredictable and meaningless to
us.

In short, I agree with Kymlicka that we can justify the protection of cultural communities at least in part on the basis of their
importance to their individual members. I have argued, more
generally, that normative communities are essential to human life

as we know it, and I would amend that argument to say that cultural communities are especially central. Thus, I would take an even stronger position than he does, namely, that without cultural communities, individuals of our species would not be *human*. It is on these grounds that I would argue that cultural communities should be entitled to protection, and that they should therefore be accorded the right to exist and maintain their integrity (the right of cultural autonomy), together with the right to be accepted as legitimate participants in the life of the country at large, participants whose characteristic attitudes and values ought to be respected even by those who do not share them (the right of cultural authority).

II

Kymlicka is concerned with the rights of indigenous, or aboriginal, minorities. What he proposes, under the rubric of minority rights, is "special measures for distinct minority cultures"; that they be accorded "special status" (LCC 139). "[I]n culturally plural societies," he says, "differential citizenship rights may be needed to protect a cultural community from unwanted disintegration." That is, "aboriginal peoples [should] have a special constitutional status that goes beyond equal rights and resources" (LCC 151–152, 182). I am prepared to support this proposal for a special status, and even, under certain circumstances, to support special measures to protect minorities that are neither indigenous nor "nations" in Kymlicka's sense but that are vulnerable and threatened by other groups or by prevalent social attitudes or practices. But Kymlicka formulates his recommendations in terms of minority *rights*, conceiving these as "special" or "differential" rights, which he contrasts with "equal citizenship rights," specified to apply to every [Canadian] citizen "without regard to race or ethnicity" (LCC 151).

Kymlicka is careful to distinguish between the differential rights he proposes and privileges, or what has come, in the United States, to be called "reverse discrimination." Here, too, he wants to modify the liberal view. "[O]n the standard interpretation of liberalism," which he opposes, "aboriginal rights are viewed as matters of discrimination and/or privilege, not of equality" (LCC 154). Kymlicka's response (which I take to be an appropriate one) is that "the special measures demanded by aboriginal people serve to correct an advantage that nonaboriginal people have before anyone makes their choices" (LCC 189). "Without special protection . . . the cultural community . . . is likely to be undermined by the decisions of people outside the community. . . . The rectification of this inequality is the basis for a liberal defence of aboriginal rights, and of minority rights in general" (LCC 189). That is, Kymlicka conceives minority rights as a form of what has been called "affirmative action."

> The English and French in Canada rarely have to worry about the fate of their cultural structure. They get for free what aboriginal people have to pay for: secure cultural membership. This is an important inequality, and if it is ignored, it becomes an important injustice. Special political rights, however, can correct this inequality by ensuring that aboriginal communities are as secure as nonaboriginal ones. . . . [S]pecial political rights are needed to remove inequalities in the context of choice which arise before people even make their choices [LCC 190].

If there are these inequalities, then justice and equal citizenship rights demand that they be removed. And if the members of a minority are denied equal treatment under the law because of their culture, this demands redress. In addition to supporting the rights of cultural autonomy and authority for communities as such, I have argued that, to ensure their equal rights as individuals, the members of every cultural group should be *collectively* entitled to equal rights and equal treatment. Because the members of any such group—or the group as a whole—could be unfairly treated on the basis of their collective identity, that identity should be the ground of a collective *right*, a right that should be not only written into law but made operative in the life of the society and in the way members of its different cultural communities behave toward one another. But these would be rights only if they were operative in principle for all those communities, even though they would have to be invoked only by or for some of them, and even if their implementation in particular cases would be impossible without the adoption of special policies or legislation.

As he acknowledges, Kymlicka's proposal does not rest on a particular theory of rights (see LCC 139). The closest I find him coming to formulating a definition of rights is in a discussion of the Canadian concept of aboriginal rights, where he implies that rights are claims that are to be respected, and that they are "trumps" outweighing other interests: "[I]t is the usual implication of that term ['aboriginal rights'] that aboriginal peoples (not Canadians generally) have rights to the protection of their culture. And what makes them *rights* is that they are claims to be respected even if some other policy would better serve the interests of the Canadian political community" (LCC 133).

Rather than conceiving them as claims or even justified claims (which are weaker than rights), I have analyzed rights as entitlements, inseparable (because the two are mutually definitive) from the correlative obligation to respect them. But this difference could be held to be merely verbal. My main point of difference with Kymlicka is that I maintain that even if measures taken to compensate for antecedent inequality are necessary, and in this sense should not be considered privileges, the nature of rights is such that the concept of "differential rights" is self-contradictory.

A right is an entitlement that we must respect, but this is not all. To be entitled to something as a matter of *right* involves a stronger condition. Entitlements as such can be granted selectively; for instance, some societies entitle men but not women to have multiple spouses. But this is to privilege those who are thus entitled. Rights, in contrast, are not privileges. They cannot be selectively denied. The normative principle governing any right confers the entitlement in question jointly with the obligation to respect it. As social institutions, rights-norms are features of the governing perspectives of actual communities and binding upon all their members. What distinguishes an entitlement as a right is that it is conferred in the same way on all who are obligated to respect it, that is, on all members of the community, who are alike expected to abide by its norms. Even more strongly, to maintain that something is a right is to mean that we would extend the same entitlement to, and expect the same respect for it from, anyone else, even to strangers, treating them as at least potentially members of our normative community of rights. Strictly speaking, the term 'equal rights' is redundant: So-called "rights" that are not accorded to all do not have the moral status of rights. This is not to say that in practice a right cannot be overridden, either by competing rights or by other compelling imperatives. But the distinction between a right and any other entitlement is that everyone who understands an entitlement to be a right, understands that he or she not only must respect it but is empowered by the norms to assert that right in his or her own person. I take this to be the import of the conventional concept of "universal rights," which extends what it means to be a right beyond the bounds of any actual community to an ideal universal community.

Rights-norms cannot always be implemented. The force of such a norm, however, empowers every member of the community in which it is operative, without exception, to exercise the entitlement it confers if and when circumstances warrant, just as it obligates all to respect that entitlement and to implement this respect—or help see that it is implemented—if and when such action is called for. That is, in the language that I have previously employed, even though they are *applicable* only when certain conditions are fulfilled, the norms prescribing rights are *relevant* to all who are expected to internalize them. That is, rights involve mutual or *symmetrical* entitlements together with mutual obligations to respect them. In contrast, the "differential rights" that Kymlicka supports are *asymmetrical* entitlements. To put it another way: they are not rights, because they lack the generality of rights. Assigned to selected cultural communities and their members, they could not be claimed by any others, even if circumstances warranted.

If Kymlicka were to argue for the rights of all cultural communities to protection in the event that they are threatened; if he were to argue that all the peoples and ethnic groups in every country ought to enjoy and respect both the right to exist and the right to cultural autonomy and legitimacy, not only would he be using the concept of rights appropriately, but he would also be providing justification for the measures necessary to ensure that any communities whose existence and identity are in jeopardy are protected. To grant sovereignty over the territory in which a particular culture is rooted and to pass laws guaranteeing that sovereignty, or to make education in their native tongue available to the children of that particular community, can be justified on the grounds that every cultural community has a right to self-preservation and, hence, when necessary, to the provision of conditions requisite for the protection of that right. But measures explicitly designed for and relevant only to a selected party or parties, measures that are in principle denied to others, are not rights. Those singled out for such "special treatment" may require it, and it may justifiably be legislated as an entitlement; but if other members of the community are *de jure* precluded from sharing it, despite its legality and its moral justification, and regardless of Kymlicka's disclaimer, that entitlement is a privilege, not a right.

NOTES

1. Zdravko Grebo, "Twenty-Five Years of Ignorance," available from Peace Action International, 866 United Nations Plaza, Room 4053, New York, New York 10017.

2. In the work on which I shall concentrate, while there is mention of the ambiguous political status of indigenous peoples under Section 35 of the 1982 Constitution Act, there is little discussion of the issue of according full citizenship rights to indigenous people. I shall discuss this problem in a subsequent chapter.

3. Will Kymlicka, *Multicultural Citizenship: A Liberal Theory of Minority Rights* (Oxford: Oxford University Press, 1995), p. 11.

4. Jay A. Sigler, *Minority Rights: A Comparative Analysis* (Westport, Connecticut: Greenwood Press, 1983), p. 5.

5. Lawrence Wright, "One Drop of Blood," *The New Yorker*, July 25, 1994, p. 50.

6. Larry May, *The Morality of Groups* (Notre Dame, Indiana: Notre Dame University Press, 1989), pp. 9, 10, 147, 180.

7. Will Kymlicka, *Liberalism, Community, and Culture* (Oxford: Clarendon Press, 1989); hereafter cited as LCC.

8. See Robert K. Merton's "Contributions to the Theory of Reference Group Behavior," in *Continuities in Social Research: Studies in the Scope and Method of the American Soldier*, ed. Robert K. Merton and Paul F. Lazarsfeld (Glencoe, Illinois: The Free Press, 1950), pp. 40–105; as well as his *Social Theory and Social Structure*, rev. ed. (Glencoe, Illinois: The Free Press, 1957).

7

Deep Diversity: Charles Taylor and the Politics of Federalism

ALTHOUGH THIS CHAPTER WILL CENTER on a concept introduced by Charles Taylor, I shall bring to bear upon it writings by a number of other Canadian scholars. Taylor—who also speaks as a political figure—is an advocate of special status for Francophones and the province of Quebec, much as his younger Canadian colleague and critic Will Kymlicka is an advocate of "special rights" and special status for aboriginal peoples. Both are part of the Anglo-European tradition and, in dealing with the Canadian situation, they address work by others in the same tradition. For instance, while the bibliography of Kymlicka's *Liberalism, Community, and Culture* lists several works by aboriginal writers, he makes few references to their positions save in notes.[1] Similarly, Taylor maintains that the constitutional changes he proposes in *Reconciling the Solitudes* will "do justice to [Canada's] aboriginal populations" as well as to Quebecers.[2] Yet he fails to take into account any writings by aboriginals or official statements issued by aboriginal organizations. As Menno Boldt, J. Anthony Long, and Leroy Little Bear charge in the Preface to their anthology, *The Quest for Justice: Aboriginal Peoples and Aboriginal Rights*, "the aboriginal perspective is largely missing from published works on issues affecting aboriginal peoples."[3] One Euro-Canadian thinker who does take aboriginal writings and documents into account is Michael Asch, an anthropologist whose book *Home and Native Land: Aboriginal Rights and the Canadian Constitution* is a penetrating essay in applied political philosophy.[4] In what follows, I shall try to bring material from this book and from *The Quest for Justice* to bear on Taylor's proposal and on its consequences for aboriginal communities as well as for Quebec.

It is common, in some parts of the world, to refer to a culturally and linguistically distinct population, particularly one that is identified with a particular geographic location, as a nation. Using the term in this sense, we can think of Francophone Quebecers as a nation, as are the aboriginal peoples, the First Nations, of Canada. English Canada, while culturally and historically distinct, has come to include many immigrant groups, who have largely assimilated English culture, and English speakers tend to think of themselves as Canadian rather than as English. While focusing on the French, Taylor, instead of advocating independence, searches for a way to allow all the diverse nations a substantial measure of self-government while still preserving Canadian unity. Despite the fact that his view of Canada as basically binational and bilingual continually surfaces, he gives us a pluralist solution. Rather than dwell on his dualist bias, I want to concentrate on this proposal, which turns out to be consonant with Asch's approach and with the view that seems to predominate in the aboriginal nations. Asch quotes Dr. David Ahenakew, national chief of the Assembly of First Nations,[5] addressing the Constitutional Conference of First Ministers in 1983: "We recognize that it is the view of many that the word 'sovereignty' defines an extreme at one end of a list of options available and the word 'assimilation' describes an extreme on the opposite end. We say there is a middle ground" (HNL 89). The complex type of federalism that Taylor advocates, incorporating the principle he calls "deep diversity," is located in that middle ground.

Boldt and Long, in the concluding paper in *The Quest for Justice*, acknowledge that some indigenous peoples have "adopted the concept of sovereignty as the cornerstone of their aspirations."[6] But they take this position to be mistaken, and point out that, historically, the European concept of sovereignty is "not relevant to their internal or external relationships." It was never "in the cultural apparatus of Indians" (TT 341, 342). ('Indian' is used by them as a generic name for the diverse aboriginal peoples.) "Prior to colonization, Indian tribes held an independent self-governing status best defined as 'nationhood,' not 'statehood' " (TT 340). Their own position, like Ahenakew's, is that "the acceptable model for a relationship between the federal government and

Canada's Indians lies somewhere between assimilation and sovereignty" (TT 342).

In the same volume, Fred Plain defends the aboriginal right of "independence through . . . self-government, our right to self-determination, . . . to nationhood."[7] The right to self-determination is, first of all, the right of each indigenous nation "to develop its own traditions and culture—its own civilization." It is a right "to develop and grow under our own system, and our own system will flow from our own people, who," Plain says, "will develop our own constitution" (QJ 33). But he goes on to claim that "[o]ur Indian constitutions have every right to be recognized in any new Canadian constitution," implying that the independence and self-government sought by his people are to be within the Canadian federation (QJ 33). He reports that, in their declaration of 1977, the Nishawbe-Aski Commission "stressed that their objective was to see the full development of cultural, economic, spiritual, and political independence" (QJ 36). Speaking of what he holds to be the original right of the Nishawbe-Aski people to their own constitution, "the right to make their own laws and determine their own destiny through their own governing system," Plain states that their challenge to the Canadian constitution was based on the government's unwillingness to recognize this right. He goes on to speak of "the true aboriginal rights that must be recognized in any Canadian constitution."

Speaking for the Inuit people, Peter Ittinuar takes a strong position in favor of federalism: "The challenge we face is to insure the preservation of [our aboriginal] rights in the context of an evolving Canadian federalism. I suspect the Indian and Metis peoples see their struggle in much the same way."[8]

What Taylor calls for is a more decentralized and more complicated federal system than that which presently obtains in Canada. He specifies that the "asymmetrical federalism" he is talking about "means special status for Quebec."[9] But in fact the kind of "deep diversity" he recommends would confer special status on each constituent, including several new political entities that would be created. That is, each might have different powers, different spheres of autonomy. He would like to see Quebec retain all its current provincial powers, but other provinces might "opt for the centralization of several powers" and while some "coordination will occur through interprovincial agreements," in certain cases "it would be better to imagine a shared or concurrent jurisdiction" (RS 147). As Taylor puts it at one point, "to each province according to its tasks," the powers that would enable it "to cope with problems . . . that other provinces do not have" (DV 180). But over and above the provinces, he recommends "the granting of certain powers of self-rule to aboriginal communities" (CR 148). Assuming that these communities are the national communities or tribes, this would mean creating a new level of political organization, neither provincial nor municipal and, in some cases, crossing provincial boundaries: "[O]ur arrangements have to accommodate the need for forms of self-government and self-management appropriate to the different First Nations. This may mean in practice allowing for a new form of jurisdiction in Canada, perhaps weaker than the provinces, but, unlike municipalities, not simply the creatures of another level of government" (DV 180).

The fundamental principle of this restructuring of the country is provision of a new basis for citizenship, reflecting the existence of diverse nations within the state.[10] Rather than accepting the view of Canada at large as a multicultural mosaic, in which ethnic origin has the same weight and significance for everyone and assimilation is expected to be the norm, Taylor introduces the concept of what he calls "second-level" or "deep" diversity and suggests a restructuring of the Canadian polity based upon it. Unlike the "first-level" diversity of the conventional model, in which one is a citizen of a country simply as an individual, the "deep diversity" model recognizes the importance of national identity and the resistance of national communities to assimilation. The aboriginal peoples are established nations with a long history and insist upon their national status at least as strongly as does the Francophone population of Quebec. He proposes, therefore, that members of these communities hold citizenship in the state, not as independent individuals, but as and insofar as they belong to the subaltern nations. Those who identify as Canadians, including the descendants of immigrants and Indians who have opted for "enfranchisement" (termination of Indian status), would hold citizenship in the country directly.[11]

Giving special citizenship status to Indians, Inuit, and Metis is consistent with the aboriginal rights guaranteed by the Constitutional Act of 1982, rights that these peoples insist belong to them as nations rather than to their members as individuals.[12] What is at stake is both the sense of identity and actual political status. "To build a country for everyone," Taylor contends,

> Canada would have to allow for second-level or "deep" diversity, in which a plurality of ways of belonging would also be acknowledged and accepted. Someone of, say, Italian extraction in Toronto or Ukrainian extraction in Edmonton might indeed feel Canadian as a bearer of individual rights in a multicultural mosaic. His or her belonging would not "pass through" some other community, although the ethnic identity might be important to him or her in various ways. But this person might nevertheless accept that a Québécois, or a Cree, or a Déné might belong in a very different way, that these persons were Canadian through being members of their national communities. Reciprocally, the Québécois, Cree, or Déné would accept the perfect legitimacy of the "mosaic identity" [DV 183].

Reminding us of the important functions performed by a federal state—everything from defense and the provision of currency to regulating "regional equality and mutual self-help"—Taylor argues for its necessity and, hence, against political independence for the constituent nations, even Quebec. "Deep diversity," he holds, is "the only formula on which a united federal Canada can be built" (DV 183). And, looking beyond Canada, he writes, "Second, in many parts of the world today the degree and nature of the differences resemble those of Canada. . . . If a uniform model of citizenship fits better the classical image of the Western liberal state, it is also true that this is a straightjacket for many political societies. The world needs other models to be legitimated in order to allow for more humane and less constraining modes of political cohabitation" (DV 183). Examples of regions in need of such a solution are too numerous to need mention.

Speculating about the role of political institutions in society, Taylor supports the principle of diversity in another respect: he proposes that political life and the form it takes, rather than being limited to the performance of a public service, can also play a part in securing unity and defining a communal identity. "The definition of the national identity of Quebeckers," he holds, can be (at least in part) a function of the democratic character of their political life, by the fact that "the nation's prime ground of agreement will be the fair and honest contest between different tendencies aspiring to determine the community's goals."[13] The same principle can be applied at a higher organizational level to Canada at large, or to any other multinational polity. Taylor restates it in an interesting way that, I think, takes us a step beyond "deep diversity." In place of "a national life presuming unanimity," he proposes an alternative "ideal type" of national identity, "a national life founded on diversity, in which the political process takes on a crucial significance, not only as an instrument of self-definition but as a major component of a national identity, which is largely constituted by debate, without definitive closure, between a plurality of legitimate options" (RS 132). This is Taylor's vision of "politics as the way of life of free citizens" (RS 131). Applied to Canada as a whole, the concept of "debate without definitive closure" opens up the possibility of a polity that provides for its own evolution, for the kind of "evolving Canadian federation" for which Ittinuar hopes.

A political life founded on diversity, in which each member of the federation would be free to evolve its own form of self-governance, would embody the kind of "politics of recognition" Taylor repeatedly advocates. It is consonant, not only with Canadian aboriginal rights as officially defined, but also with what Boldt and Long hold to be the aspiration of most native peoples:

> Most Indian peoples are committed to a separate social system with corresponding networks of social institutions that are congruent with their historical tribal arrangements and that are based on their traditional identity, language, religion, philosophy, and customs. The Canadian government is ready to accept Indian self-government. The challenge for Indian leaders is to develop a model of self-government that is acceptable to the Canadian government and that gives Indians internal self-determination without compromising fundamental traditional values. The option of pluralism suggests itself [TT 342].

Among these traditional values is direct participatory democracy and rule by consensus. While majority rule might still be the norm in Canada at large, indigenous tribes could still govern themselves internally in their traditional way, in which "the people ruled collectively, exercising authority as one body with undivided power, performing all functions of government" (TT 337).[14]

In *Home and Native Land*, Michael Asch advocates a version of "consociationism," a concept of political pluralism explored independently by two different Western thinkers, Arend Lijphart and M. G. Smith, and versions of which are typified by Belgium and Switzerland.[15] Holding that it is possible to incorporate such a system within the Canadian political state, Asch maintains that it can accommodate both "the aboriginal fact" and "the French fact" (HNL 82). It is also in line with the expressed views of the Assembly of First Nations, which include

> a division of responsibilities between a national and a segmental level; a land base upon which to establish the legislative authority deemed essential to insure the autonomous development of the segment; the protection of segmental rights through the introduction of a veto over changes that otherwise might be imposed by the other segments of the population; and some degree of proportionality in representation. As such, it is a position that reflects, in its specific goals as well as in its overall orientation, consistency with the principles of consecration . . . [HNL 89].

Proportional representation is one way to ensure that the interests of the smaller aboriginal nations are taken into account. Protection of each nation's land base is especially important because of the close association in aboriginal thought between identity, community, and location. As Paul Tennant puts it, in his article in *The Quest for Justice*,

> In keeping with aboriginal philosophy, Indian claims are invariably advanced on behalf of the community. Indians take the position that their claims to land and self-government do not depend on racial criteria or particular cultural elements, but rather on the existence of their communities from time immemorial. . . .
>   'Place' is the key element; it implies and includes the claim to continued functioning of the community in that place, and self-government is a key function of this functioning.[16]

The most important element in consociational democracy, Asch points out, is that "citizenship presumes identification with one

or the other of the primary ethnonational collectivities . . . each
[of which] bears coordinate status" (HNL 78). (Taylor's model
would conform if all the collectivities had comparable status.)

Comparing aboriginal designs for self-governance and relating
them to the consociational view, Asch finds two main groups of
proposals. Those of the southern tribes, who are minorities in
their areas, are much closer to the "direct" consociational model
exemplified by Belgium: selected areas of jurisdiction would,
through explicit legislation, be placed under segmental control
("direct entrenchment"). "That is, the ethnonational political
rights of the aboriginal peoples would be specified and guaranteed
to a named ethnonational entity: the aboriginal peoples of Canada." However, "it is anticipated that whereas the powers to be
acquired through entrenchment will be specified, different groups
will shape their institutions of government in different ways"
(HNL 90, 91–92).

The northern peoples, reflecting the fact that each constitutes a
majority or near majority of the population of its home territory,
have called for two separate, self-governing jurisdictions, Nunavut and Denendeh, each with power over its own culture and
resources. But their proposals, too, differ from one another. The
Inuit proposal for Nunavut is much more like the present provincial governments and closer to the "indirect" consociational
model, relying on the vote of all the citizens. This was expressed
by the Nunavut Constitutional Forum in 1983: "Nunavut is
'public government'. That is, it is a government for all the people
who live in the area embraced by Nunavut whether they were
born in Igloolik or Trois Rivières, Lloydminster or Yellowknife.
Nunavut is not a government only for Inuit, but a government
firmly founded on the Canadian political tradition of public services and the power of participation for all people who live in a
geographical area" (HNL 94).

Nevertheless, according to the same document, the Nunavut
government would "provide specific guarantees for Inuit in respect of certain of their vital interests. . . . Nunavut will not only
be a provincial-type government, but also the homeland of the
distinct and ancient Inuit culture," with a special role in protecting the Inuit heritage (HNL 94). The Dene and Metis proposal
for Denendeh would accomplish a similar end by means of a

Charter of Founding Principles, which would provide for "the right of the Dene (and other citizens) to 'establish government funded institutions and services to reflect their respective values and ways, in such areas as education, health services, and social services'" (HNL 98, 97). And, to protect their majority status, since outsiders tend to come to the Northwest Territories for relatively short periods in connection with employment, both nations would impose a longer residency requirement for voting than the other provinces do (HNL 102–103).

That Taylor's proposal for a federalism based on deep diversity would, in the main, be found congenial by these writers seems likely. However, concerning all the ideas considered here, let me paraphrase Asch's conclusion regarding the proposals for Nunavut and Denendeh: "Although they are foreign to our traditional political culture, [they do not seem] to produce a situation that is at variance with our fundamental political values"; but they require "a degree of flexibility in organizing institutions of government" beyond what anyone has yet achieved (HNL 104).

NOTES

1. Will Kymlicka, *Liberalism, Community, and Culture* (Oxford: Clarendon Press, 1989). In his more recent book, *Multicultural Citizenship: A Liberal Theory of Minority Rights* (Oxford: Oxford University Press, 1995), he cites a paper, "Native Rights as Collective Rights: A Question of Group Self-Preservation," *Canadian Journal of Law and Jurisprudence*, 2, No. 1 (1989), by an aboriginal philosopher, Darlene M. Johnston, in a note on the concept of collective rights, identifying it as representative of "the 'communitarian' camp" (p. 207*n*20). This paper is included in the anthology Kymlicka edited, *The Rights of Minority Cultures* (Oxford: Oxford University Press, 1995), pp. 179–201.

2. Charles Taylor, "Shared and Divergent Values" (1991) in *Reconciling the Solitudes: Essays on Canadian Federalism and Nationalism*, ed. Guy LaForest (Montreal and Kingston: McGill-Queens University Press, 1993), p. 184. Hereafter, the chapter will be cited as DV; the volume, which is a collection of independent papers and addresses, as RS.

3. *The Quest for Justice: Aboriginal Peoples and Aboriginal Rights*, ed. Menno Boldt and J. Anthony Long, in association with Leroy Little Bear (Toronto: University of Toronto Press, 1985); hereafter cited as QJ.

4. Michael Asch, *Home and Native Land: Aboriginal Rights and the Canadian Constitution* (Vancouver: University of British Columbia Press, 1993); hereafter cited as HNL. Another writer who takes the views of aboriginals into account is Allan McChesney; see his "Aboriginal Communities, Aboriginal Rights, and the Human Rights System in Canada," in *Human Rights in Cross-Cultural Perspective: A Quest for Consensus*, ed. Abdullah Ahmed An-Na'im (Philadelphia: University of Pennsylvania Press, 1992).

5. The Assembly of First Nations represents reservation Indians; off-reservation Indians are represented by the Native Council of Canada.

6. Menno Boldt and J. Anthony Long, "Tribal Traditions and European-Western Political Ideologies: The Dilemma of Canada's Native Indians" (QJ 333); hereafter cited as TT.

7. Fred Plain, "A Treatise on the Rights of the Aboriginal Peoples of the Continent of North America" (QJ 32).

8. Peter Ittinuar, "The Inuit Perspective on Aboriginal Rights" (QJ 47). Metis are of mixed Indian and non-Indian heritage.

9. Taylor, "The Stakes of Constitutional Reform" (1990), RS 150; hereafter cited as CR.

10. Cf. Kymlicka's contention that differential citizenship rights may be needed in culturally plural societies, Chapter 6, p. 103 above.

11. 'Enfranchisement' has a special usage in Canada, unrelated to the vote: "The term 'enfranchisement' is another misnomer perpetuated by the Indian Act. Indians can vote in all elections in Canada [since 1960]. Termination of status does not alter voting rights" (Douglas Sanders, "The Bill of Rights and Indian Status," *University of British Columbia Law Review*, 7, No. 1 [1965], 94*n*6).

12. Pertaining only to selected groups, these are not rights in my sense of the term.

13. Taylor, "Institutions in National Life" (1988) (RS 130).

14. Boldt and Long acknowledge the fact that this concept is inconsistent with the European notion of sovereignty, with its sharp distinction between the ruler and the ruled (TT 337).

15. Arend Lijphart, *Democracy in Plural Societies* (New Haven, Connecticut: Yale University Press, 1977); M. G. Smith, "Some Developments in the Analytic Framework of Pluralism," in *Pluralism in Africa*, ed. Leo Kuper and M. G. Smith (Berkeley: University of California Press, 1969), pp. 415–458.

16. Paul Tennant, "Aboriginal Rights and the Penner Report on Indian Self-Government" (QJ 324).

III
DEMOCRATIC PRAXIS

8

Pragmatism, Rights, and Democracy*

JOHN DEWEY IS WELL KNOWN for his writings on democracy, but after 1920, his references to rights were largely critical, and it is widely assumed that Pragmatism is antithetical to the assertion of rights. However, Dewey's criticisms were largely directed at particular features of traditional theories of rights, not against rights as such, and there is to be found, in his earlier writings, a positive conception of rights. But the most important pragmatist theory of rights, and one that has also received very little attention, was developed by George Herbert Mead. After discussing their views on key aspects of both rights and democracy, I shall draw some implications for our understanding of the democratic process.[1]

DEWEY

One of Dewey's criticisms of the dominant view of rights is a repudiation of the individualism of natural rights theories. Significantly, he not only rejects the conventional view but puts forth a positive suggestion, "an assertion of the rights of groups."[2] However, Dewey's rejection of individualism is coupled with a stress on the importance of individuality. This stress is central to *Individualism Old and New*, where he argues that "[a]ssured and integrated individuality is the product of definite social relationships and publicly acknowledged functions."[3] But Dewey insisted that "[t]he development of a civilization that is outwardly corporate—or rapidly becoming so—has been accompanied by a sub-

---

*This chapter was originally presented as an invited paper at the annual meeting of the Eastern Division of the American Philosophical Association, December 29, 1995.

mergence of the individual" (ION 66). The result, for the individual, is "the absence of a sense of social value" (ION 67) Moreover, the economic insecurity of his time was such that "[f]ear of loss of work, [and] dread of the oncoming of old age, create anxiety and eat into self-respect in a way that impairs personal dignity," so that "courageous and robust individuality is undermined" (*Individualism* 68). Hence, his conclusion that a "stable recovery of individuality waits upon an elimination of the older economic and political individualism . . ." (ION 75–76).

This political individualism was integral to the traditional concept of "natural rights," which Dewey rejected on other (though not unrelated) grounds. Like the British philosopher T. H. Green, about whom he had written (albeit critically), Dewey took the concept of "antecedent" rights, prior to membership in society, to be "a fiction."[4] But this view does not entail the belief that rights as such are fictional and, as we shall see, Dewey considered rights to be important features of social institutions. In a lecture on political liberalism, one of a series he gave in China in 1919 and 1920, Dewey stressed the importance of the right of suffrage, and then said,

> It is worthwhile to emphasize again the point I have already made a number of times, namely, that the rights and powers we are discussing have no meaning if we choose to consider the individual apart from the society and the state. The individual can have these rights only so long as he is a member of his society and his state; there are no such things as individual rights until and unless they are supported and maintained by society, through law.[5]

The principle underlying this view is expressed in a 1928 essay: "[A]ctual, that is, effective, rights and demands are products of interactions, and are not found in the original and isolated constitution of human nature, whether moral or psychological. . . ."[6] Dewey saw the idea that rights are independent of membership in society as having its source in the struggle for liberation from oppressive governments. The same factor accounts for the individualism of the prevailing rights theories. "Thus," he says, "the practical movement for the limitation of the powers of government became associated, as in the influential philosophy of John Locke, with the doctrine that the ground and justification of the restriction was prior non-political rights inherent in the very structure of the individual" (PP 289). But concerning this individualism, Dewey went on to say:

> It is now easy for the imagination to conceive circumstances under which revolts against prior governmental forms would have found its [sic] theoretical formulation in an assertion of the rights of groups, of other associations than those of a political nature. There was no logic which rendered necessary the appeal to the individual as an independent and isolated being [PP 289].

That is, in opposition to the view that predominates even today, Dewey suggests that there can be collective or group rights as well as rights of individuals.

In his very early *Outlines of a Critical Theory of Ethics*, Dewey had broadened the scope of rights in yet other ways: "Every institution," he says there,

> has its sovereignty, or authority, and its laws and rights. It is only a false abstraction which makes us conceive of sovereignty, or authority, and of law and of rights as inhering only in some supreme organization, as the national state. The family, the school, the neighborhood group, has its authority as respects its members, imposes its ideals of action, or laws, and confers its respective satisfactions in way of enlarged freedom, or rights.[7]

Institutions and, consequently, rights are said by him to be the expression of a common will. It is "the activity of the common will," "the public reason," that "gives freedom, or *rights*, to the various members of the institution" (CTE 347–348). He defines rights as powers of action that one gets as a member of a community, "powers which are not mere claims, nor simply claims recognized by others, but claims reinforced by the will of the whole community" (CTE 349). The sovereignty and authority of any institution, however, are understood by Dewey at this time (under the influence of Hegel) to be subordinate to those of the more comprehensive organization to which it belongs, and he takes all other sovereignty and authority to be relative to that of humanity: "Only humanity or the organized activity of all the wants, powers and interests common to men, can have absolute sovereignty, law and rights" (CTE 348). At the same time, he contends that without local authorities, rights, and laws, "humanity would be a meaningless abstraction, and its activity wholly empty" (CTE 348).

In Chapter 20 of the original (1908) version of the book on ethics he wrote with James H. Tufts, a chapter of which Dewey himself is the author, Section Three is entitled, "Rights and Obligations." In this section, Dewey analyzes rights in terms of the reciprocal roles of the individual agent and society and in terms of obligations as well as freedom:

> a right, individual in residence, is social in origin and intent. The social factor in rights is made explicit in the demand that the power in question be exercised in certain ways. A right is never a claim to a wholesale, indefinite activity, but to a *defined* activity; *to one carried on*, that is, *under certain conditions*. This limitation constitutes the *obligatory* phase of every right. . . . Rights and obligations are thus strictly correlatives.[8]

The section goes on to classify the rights that individuals have or ought to have, and the next chapter, also written by Dewey, goes into greater detail concerning civil and political rights and obligations and democracy. "[T]he representative and potential significance of political rights," he says, "exceeds that of any other class of rights." He continues: "Suffrage stands for direct and active participation in the regulation of the terms upon which associated life shall be sustained, and the pursuit of the good carried on. Political freedom and responsibility *express an individual's power and obligation to make effective all his other capacities by fixing the social conditions of their exercise.*"[9]

Concerning the growth of democracy, Dewey says,

> The evolution of democratically regulated States, as distinct from those ordered in the interests of a small group, or of a special class, is the social counterpart of the development of a comprehensive and common good. Externally viewed, democracy is a piece of machinery, to be maintained or thrown away, like any other piece of machinery, on the basis of its economy and efficiency of working. Morally, it is the effective embodiment of the moral ideal of a good which consists in the development of all the social capacities of every individual member of society.[10]

As in the later *Individualism Old and New*, Dewey here places a high value on individuality and for this very reason criticizes "the individualistic formula." The "moral criterion" by which he would evaluate social institutions and political measures is whether they "set free individual capacities in such a way as to make them available for the development of the general happiness or the common good." Stated with reference to society, he says, the test is "whether the general, the public, organization and order are promoted in such a way as to equalize opportunity for all." What Dewey has in mind here is each individual's "whole system of capacities and activities," his "concrete freedom." In contrast with "[t]he maximum freedom of one individual consistent with equal *concrete* or total freedom of others," he construes the individualistic or "*laissez-faire*" principle, "the maximum possible freedom of the individual consistent with his not interfering with like freedom on the part of other individuals," to refer to "only an abstract, mechanical, external, and hence formal freedom."[11]

Even in the revised 1932 edition of the *Ethics*, which omits the chapters on rights included in the original edition, certain rights are identified and discussed, some of them by Dewey.[12] Most important is what he says about the liberty of thought and expression:

> Liberty to think, inquire, discuss, is central in the whole group of rights which are secured in theory to individuals in a democratic social organization. It is central because the essence of the democratic principle is appeal to voluntary disposition instead of to force, to persuasion instead of coercion. . . . Free circulation of intelligence is not enough barely of itself to effect the success of democratic institutions. But apart from it there is no opportunity either for the formation of a common judgment and purpose or for the voluntary participation of individuals in the affairs of government. For the only alternative to control by thought and conviction is control by externally applied force, or at best by unquestioned custom [1932 *Ethics* 358].

The interdependence of rights and democracy is thus a continuing motif in Dewey's opus.

Voicing a theme more widely associated with him, Dewey repeatedly distinguishes between democracy as a form of government and democracy as a form of social life.[13] There is a sense in which democratic government—by which he means the mechanisms of representative democracy, such as universal suffrage and majority rule—is a means to the end of democratic social life. But, in an essay entitled "Democracy Is Radical," Dewey also speaks of the latter as itself a means to "the ends of liberty and individuality."[14] Developing this idea, he says:

> [D]emocracy means not only the ends [of] security for individuals and opportunity for their development as personalities. It signifies also primary emphasis upon the *means* by which these ends are to be fulfilled. The means to which it is devoted are the voluntary activities of individuals in opposition to coercion; they are assent and consent in opposition to violence; they are the force of intelligent organization versus that of organization imposed from outside and above. *The fundamental principle of democracy is that the ends of freedom and individuality for all can be attained only by means that accord with those ends* [DR 298].

The democratic end is "radical," Dewey contends, because "*it is an end that has not been adequately realized in any country at any time.*" And there is "nothing more radical than insistence upon democratic methods"—in place of reliance on physical force, which Dewey characterizes as "the reactionary position"—"as the means by which radical social changes be effected" (DR 299). Faith in democracy, which, in this essay, Dewey is arguing for in opposition to both "German Nazi-socialism" and the dictatorship of the proletariat advocated by "the rulers of Soviet Russia," must spring "from a living faith in our common human nature and in the power of voluntary action based upon public collective intelligence" (DR 299).

Dewey's position regarding the means to the democratic end was radical in another sense, as is well known. While he identified his own view with liberalism, in economics he defended a form of socialism. Nevertheless, he described socialism in what he took to be democratic terms. "[L]et those who are struggling to replace the present economic system by a cooperative one," he argued, those who are "struggling for a more equal and equitable balance of powers that will enhance and multiply the effective liberties of the mass of individuals . . . not be jockeyed into the position of supporting social control at the expense of liberty, when what they want is another method of social control than the one that

now exists, one that will increase significant human liberties."[15]
The "means" he described were intended to provide such a
method of democratic social control. The contrast between this
description and his earlier characterization, in *Liberalism and Social
Action*, of "organized social control of economic forces" as "regi-
mentation of material and mechanical forces" should not be over-
looked.[16] Yet, in the same book, Dewey describes "[t]he method
of democracy" for resolving "conflicts of class interest" as follows:

> The problem . . . is precisely how conflicting claims are to be
> settled in the interest of the widest possible contribution to the
> interests of all—or at least of the great majority. The method of
> democracy—inasfar as it is that of organized intelligence—is to
> bring these conflicts out into the open where their special claims
> can be seen and appraised, where they can be discussed and judged
> in the light of more inclusive interests than are represented by ei-
> ther of them separately [LSA 56].

The examples he gives of such conflicts are the "clash of interests
between munition manufacturers and most of the rest of the population" and between "finance-capitalism that controls the means
of production and whose profit is served by maintaining relative
scarcity, and idle workers and hungry consumers." In each case,
the "experimentalist," who would employ the method of organized intelligence in the resolution of such conflicts of interest,
"would see to it that the method depended upon by all in some
degree in every democratic community be followed through to
completion" (LSA 56).

The experimental method of organized intelligence, which
Dewey takes to be the method of democracy, is that of coopera-

tive problem-solving, which, he argues, must be engaged in by an informed, educated public such as we have yet to see. Thus, he takes his own prescription for democracy and majority rule to be "experimental" as well: "Until secrecy, prejudice, bias, misrepresentation, and propaganda as well as sheer ignorance are replaced by inquiry and publicity, we have no way of telling how apt for judgment of social policies the existing intelligence of the masses may be" (PP 366). But his basic faith is that a "more intelligent state of social affairs, one more informed with knowledge, more directed by intelligence . . . would raise the level upon which the intelligence of all operates." "The height of this level," he says, "is much more important for judgment of public concerns than are differences in intelligence quotients" (PP 366–367).

MEAD

While Mead's view of rights is consonant with that of Dewey, the two are far from identical, and Mead's approach to the subject, grounded in his social psychology and theory of communicative interaction and social control, differs greatly from Dewey's. And whereas Dewey's conception of rights seems to have been influenced by T. H. Green, who was himself strongly influenced by Jean-Jacques Rousseau, Mead builds directly on insights gained from the latter. Mead did not write extensively on the topic of human rights, and much of what he did write is embedded in works primarily devoted to other subjects. Among these are a few sections of *Mind, Self, and Society* and two essays, "The Psychology of Punitive Justice" and "National-Mindedness and International-Mindedness." His essay "Natural Rights and the Theory of the Political Institution" is the one that is most clearly focused, not only on the history of the concept of rights and criticism of the traditional natural-rights theories, but on the question of what a right is and what it means for it to exist.[18]

The heart of Mead's view is not only that rights rest on acknowledgment, recognition, but also that in claiming a right we are at the same time attributing it to others. Rights, that is, despite their seeming adversarial character, are mutual: "What are our rights in which we defend ourselves against all comers, but the rights which we recognize in others, that ours may be recognized by others?" (NM 357). And Mead holds our very individuality and identity to be constituted by "our rights and our privileges" as well as by our other traits. Together with those rights, this identity is a product of "the social structure by which we realized ourselves" (NM 356–357). Thus, for Mead, as for T. H. Green, rights are "natural," in the sense that they are social products, not in the sense of being innate properties.[19] But the source of this view, as of his understanding of rights as mutual, is Mead's interpretation of Rousseau's concept of the "general will," according to which every citizen, as "both subject and sovereign," both authorizes and is ready to obey the laws of society. Mead's version of this concept is broader than Rousseau's, however: what he calls "the attitude of the generalized other," the attitude of a community, is not limited to political communities. It is the controlling perspective shared by all the members of a community and encompassing not only laws and formal rules but all the institutionalized directives and prescriptions by which they govern their social behavior and communication.

The importance of this concept, especially with regard to rights, is not only that the attitude of the generalized other is common to all members of the community, but that to share it is to have the same attitude toward all, including oneself; it is to have the same expectations of each and to hold all to have the same responsibilities, to recognize them as having the same rights and the same obligation to respect them. It is also to share the same understandings and to know to use the same gestures and symbols in communication. In terms of Mead's pragmatist theory of meaning, in which the meaning of any action or expression is the response it calls for, the meaning of a rights claim is not only the expected acknowledgment of it, but also the expectation that this acknowledgment will be shared and the right will be implemented by anyone appropriately called upon and able to do so. Having the attitude governing rights thus enables one to play both roles in their enactment: to know to assert them and also to know that one is expected to respond as prescribed to such an assertion—roles jointly defined by the same general attitude. In either position or role, one must recognize that it applies in the same way to oneself and to others, so that, whether claiming or respecting a right, one is acknowledging that all alike have that right and are obligated to respect one another's claim to it. Thus, to say "I have a right" must be understood to mean, not that I have a claim against you or against the government, but that we have a mutual obligation, that "you and all others have the same right as I do, and I have the same responsibility to respect your right as you have to respect mine." The role of government is only instrumental: it is to enforce implementation of the rights with which the citizens are jointly and mutually endowed by the laws and other norms by which they are expected to govern themselves. Political institutions, Mead holds, are among "the tools and implements of the community," especially necessary in a large community where physical and social distance necessitates more formal means of social control than that afforded by the attitude of the generalized other alone (PI 167).

Depending on recognition for their existence, rights cannot be universal in the sense in which we customarily use this term; that they are determined by the attitude of a community implies that they are operative only among those who share that attitude and are thereby members of the community. But Mead takes this to mean that the rights recognized by a community are at least *potentially* universal.[20] The Rousseauan general will and, by implication, Mead's generalized other "presupposes that the very form of the will which man exercises is universal, that is, a man wills something only in so far as he puts himself in the place of everyone else in the community and in so far as he accepts the obligations which that act of will carries with it."[21] Mead illustrates this principle of universality with the case of property. Expressing the will of the community, which governs the institution of property and determines what we mean by this term, "the individual wills his control over his property only in so far as he wills the same sort of control for everyone else over property."[22]

Mead recognizes that both our commonsense understanding of rights and our legal practice fail to reflect the mutuality that he holds to characterize them. He explains this partly by appeal to the fact that the modern concept of rights emerged out of assertions of individual freedom against the arbitrary restraints of government (to which Dewey also calls attention). But he also holds the distorted, "negative" (i.e., adversarial) understanding of the nature of rights to be a consequence of criminal violations of established rights and our hostility to the violators.

> Wherever rights exist, invasion of those rights may be punished, and a definition of these institutions is formulated in protecting the right against trespass. The definition is again the voice of the community as a whole proclaiming and penalizing the one whose conduct has placed him under the ban. . . . [T]he law speaking against the criminal gives the sanction of the sovereign authority of the community to the negative definition of the right. It is defined in terms of its contemplated invasion [PJ 225–226].

On the other hand, Mead's assertion of the inherent mutuality of rights is supported by his contention that rights represent a common interest, the interest of the community in protecting the interests of its members. "It is the *common interest* on the part of society or those who constitute society in that which is the right of the individual which gives that right its recognition, and gives the ground for the enforcement of the right" (PI 162). Against the prevailing individualism and the belief that we are all self-seeking egoists, he cites Kant, Hegel, and Mill in support of the contention that "the individual in society does in large measure pursue ends which are not private, but are in his own mind public goods and his own good because they are public goods," and says, "Here we have a basis for a doctrine of rights which can be natural rights without the assumption of the existence of the individual and his right prior to society" (PI 163). According to this positive doctrine, "Insofar as the end is a common good, the community recognizes the individual's end as a right because it is also the good of all, and will enforce that right in the interest of all" (PI 163). In the face of the violation of rights, however, commitment to the common interest is lost, along with the positive conception of rights as jointly or mutually possessed:

> The individual who is defending his own rights against the trespasser is led to state even his family and more general social interests in abstract individualistic terms. Abstract individualism and a negative conception of liberty in terms of the freedom from restraints become the working ideas in the community. . . . The evenhandedness of justice is that of universal conscription against a common

enemy, and that of the abstract definition of rights which places the
ban upon anyone who falls outside of its rigid terms [PJ 226].

The negative and individualist definition of rights is "abstract" in
part because it takes into account only one aspect of what it means
to have a right, the liberty to do something without interference.
It omits the factors that account for the existence of rights in the
first place—people's recognition of the object of the right as a
common good and their consequent acknowledgment of it as a
right for all of them. Mead also charges the negative definition
of rights with being an expression of abstract individualism, of a
conception of the individual abstracted from social relations and
social interaction. Like Dewey, in rejecting individualism Mead is
not denying the importance of individuality. In fact, he criticizes
blanket hostility toward lawbreakers—as well as blanket approval
of those who are law abiding—on the grounds that such hostility
ignores individuating factors (one of the reasons that it leads to a
distorted conception of rights). "Just in proportion as we organize
by hostility," he says, "do we suppress individuality" (PJ 228).
Interestingly, he goes on to illustrate this with the case of party
politics: "In a political campaign that is fought on party lines the
members of the party surrender themselves to the party. They
become simply members of the party whose conscious aim is to
defeat the rival organization. For this purpose the party member
becomes merely a Republican or a Democrat" (PJ 228). When
it is confined to the purpose of defeating the rival, Mead takes
"organization through the common attitude of hostility" to be
"normal and effective." But, he notes, "as long as the social organization is dominated by the attitude of hostility the individuals
or groups who are the objectives of this organization will remain
enemies" (PJ 228).

Nevertheless, Mead calls attention to history, in the course of
which "these attitudes take on new forms as they gather new
social contents."

> The hostilities . . . have changed as men came to realize the com-
> mon whole within which these deadly struggles were fought out.
> Through rivalries, competitions, and cooperations [Mead takes
> economic relations to typify all three] men achieved the conception
> of a social state in which they asserted themselves while they at the

same time affirmed the status of the others, on the basis not only of common rights and privileges but also on the basis of differences of interest and function, in an organization of more varied individuals [PJ 229].

In *Mind, Self, and Society*, such a society is identified as a democracy, as in Rousseau's conception "of a society in which the individual maintains himself as a citizen only to the degree that he recognizes the rights of everyone else to belong to the same community" and "is able to realize himself by recognizing others as belonging to the same political organization as himself" (MSS 286–287). And he saw the same democratic principle to be embodied at a different level in the League of Nations, "where every community recognizes every other community in the very process of asserting itself." Like the individual citizen, "[t]he smallest community is in a position to express itself just because it recognizes the right of every other nation to do the same" (MSS 287). And Mead took democracy in this sense to be, like rights, at least potentially, "universal."

Like Dewey, Mead sees democracy as a form of social life rather than merely a form of government, but he interprets this view in terms of his own theory of community and communication. Linking the concept to that of Rousseau's "general will" and his own "attitude of the generalized other," Mead says that "democracy, in the sense here relevant, is an attitude," one "which goes with the universal relations of brotherhood" and in terms of which "[e]very individual [would] stand on the same level with every other." He believes this attitude to be shared by what he terms "the universal religions." In the sphere of politics, it "can get its expression only in such a form as that of democracy" (MSS 286). Fully expressed, this attitude would ensure the achievement of mutual self-realization through functional differentiation, "in which the individual realizes himself in others through that which he does as peculiar to himself" (MSS 289). Somewhat more tentatively, he says, in a subsequent section,

One may say that the attainment of that functional differentiation and social participation in the full degree is a sort of ideal which lies before the human community. The present stage of it is presented in the ideal of democracy. . . . [T]he implication of democracy is

. . . that the individual can be as highly developed as lies within the possibilities of his own inheritance, and still can enter into the attitudes of others whom he affects [MSS 326].

The model of the universal community, for Mead, is that of a universal community of discourse, such as is provided by logical discourse, in which every individual, having the same understanding of a set of "significant symbols" or "gestures," in communicating his or her own intent takes the attitude of the others (i.e., the attitude of the generalized other). This is at one and the same time "the ideal of communication" and that of democracy: "If communication can be carried through and made perfect, then there would exist the kind of democracy to which we have referred, in which each individual would carry just the response in himself that he knows he calls out in the community" (MSS 327).

In short, with the development of a democratic community and the attitude shared by its members, each individual both develops a unique self and comes more fully to understand and identify with the others. Mead compares this form of social organization with that which preceded it, an organization characterized by caste divisions such as those "between the fighting man and the rest of the community . . . the governing as over against the governed, which made it impossible for the individual of that particular group to identify himself with the others, or the others to identify themselves with him." These immutable differences the democratic order "undertakes to wipe out," and to the extent that it succeeds, they cease to be societal determinants of selfhood or grounds for identification and self-identification (MSS 318–319). And in the kind of society Mead characterizes as a political democracy, not only is every individual "to stand on the same level with every other," but also, as has already been noted, "the individual maintains himself as a citizen only to the degree that he recognizes the rights of everyone else to belong to the same community" (MSS 286).

THE POLITICS OF DEMOCRACY

Both Dewey and Mead distinguish between a democratic system of government and democracy as a form of social life. Dewey's

concept of the method of democracy and Mead's analysis of democracy in terms of communication serve to connect them: The
operations of government, particularly the workings of a legislature, no less than everyday social life, can exemplify what Mead
took to be a democratic process of communicative interaction
and, in that process, employ what Dewey called the method of
democracy. The interaction that takes place can be called the politics of democracy—"politics" in the sense of the process by which
the affairs of a community are controlled and directed.

The kind of politics to which most of us who live in democratic
states are accustomed is the "hostile" sort that Mead associates
with party politics and that also characterizes the operation of
what Dewey calls abstract or *laissez-faire* individualism, where, as
David Miller says, "individuals are expected to act instrumentally
in pursuit of their [own] interests rather than to search for common ends."[23] Miller calls this sort of politics "politics as interest-
aggregation" because it is designed to achieve a settlement in
which "a multitude of conflicting interests are aggregated into
one single outcome." Typically, this outcome is arrived at "by a
majority vote of the constituency in question" and, Miller contends, "what will happen is that individuals and groups will bar-
gain with one another until a compromise policy emerges that
commands the support of at least 51 per cent of the constituency"
(MSC 254). Especially when what is at issue is a matter that is
seriously contested, this method of bargaining and majority rule
is likely to result in a situation in which a significant portion of
the constituency does not support the compromise and is not
convinced of its value.

Miller is not the first to raise questions about the principle of
majority rule. "Majority rule, just as majority rule," Dewey says
in *The Public and Its Problems*, "is as foolish as its critics charge it
with being." "But," he continues, "it never is *merely* majority
rule." He quotes Samuel J. Tilden as saying, "The means by
which a majority comes to be a majority is the more important
thing."[24] The means that Dewey prescribes are "antecedent de-
bates, modification of views to meet the opinions of minorities,
the relative satisfaction given the latter by the fact that it has had
a chance and that next time it may be successful in becoming a
majority." And, subsequently, he says, "The essential need . . . is

the improvement of the methods and conditions of debate, discussion and persuasion" (PP 365).

In contrast to the adversarial model of democratic politics he has described, Miller recommends what he calls "politics as dialogue":

> According to this conception, people enter politics with conflicting opinions about what ought to be done over matters of general concern. What then ensues is a process of persuasion in the course of which spokesmen for the different points of view articulate reasons for the beliefs that they hold. A dialogue develops within which people may be led to revise their original opinions radically. Arguments are trumped by better arguments, until eventually a consensus emerges. . . . The important point is that people's adherence to the consensus view does not depend on its proximity to their original opinion, nor on strategic considerations, but on the strength of the arguments that have been offered for it. Once consensus is reached, it is formally adopted as common policy [MSC 255].

Politics of this kind, which Dewey would characterize as cooperative problem-solving or cooperative inquiry, would resemble the rational method of inquiry operative in the sciences and other academic disciplines. It should be possible to design a set of procedural rules to facilitate its operation in the political sphere and in government. Part of what it would require is the widespread dissemination of information and the encouragement of public discussion as well as the liberty of thought and expression guaranteed by the American Bill of Rights, all of which Dewey holds to be presupposed by democracy. But it also presupposes—and, perhaps, could also serve as a means of cultivating—the kind of mutual recognition and individual self-realization Mead finds to characterize and to be fostered by democratic social relations and communication.

Using the term 'community' in an honorific sense, Dewey identifies community with democratic community. I have defined it more broadly in terms of shared perspectives or attitudes, however rudimentary or informal these may be. In this sense, even the members of an undemocratic community or an unrelated set of individuals who yet have a common outlook constitute a community in what I take to be the generic sense—a perspectival community. What Mead calls "the attitude of a generalized other," I take to be a special kind of perspective, one constituted by a set of social norms—of rules, assumptions, and expectations regarding behaviors and responses to them—that has come to govern interaction and communication among a multiplicity of individuals. Sharing such a normative perspective binds them together in what I call a 'normative community'. But not every such community is a democratic one either. The members of a cult, for instance, who are all ready to do the bidding of a leader and expect one another to do likewise rather than determine democratically how they should conduct their common affairs, constitute a community in virtue of this commitment, which provides the normative perspective by which they govern their own behavior and their expectations regarding one another's behavior. Yet, the ideal of community that Mead projects, which is an ideal of democracy, is essentially the perfect embodiment and operation of the sharing of perspective that makes mutual understanding and communicative interaction possible and which governs mutual respect for one another's rights.

In a related vein, Dewey speaks of the method of democracy as that "of a positive toleration which amounts to sympathetic regard for the intelligence and personality of others, even if they hold views opposed to ours, and of scientific inquiry into facts and testing of ideas" (1932 *Ethics* 329). The juxtaposition of toleration and scientific inquiry is important. As noted earlier, Dewey holds the method of democracy to be "experimental." Like the method of science, it is a method of cooperative inquiry, a joint search for solutions that can be publicly validated. Dewey contrasts it with "the method of appeal to authority and to precedent" (1932 *Ethics* 329). The members of the scientific community are at one in their adherence to the scientific method, which is not simply the method of hypothesis or the method of experiment, but also a cooperative undertaking in which all hypotheses and experiments, all reasoning, assumptions, and conclusions, are open to public scrutiny and reflectively criticized and evaluated. That is, the perspective of the scientific community is what Dewey would characterize as a democratic one.

As such, it is an attitude of "*positive* toleration," by which I think Dewey means an attitude of mutual acceptance and readiness to consider one another's judgments as seriously—and as critically—as one considers one's own. To put it in terms closer to Mead's: a democratic community would be what I have called "a community of 'dialogic reciprocity'."[25] In addition to sharing a set of norms that enable them to communicate meaningfully with one another, the members of such a community accept one another as legitimate and authoritative participants in collective decision making. Not only does this community have a perspective in which rights are mutually recognized, but it is one in which two specific rights are jointly operative. These are a right of personal autonomy—the freedom to form one's own, independent judgments—and a right of personal authority—entitlement to a voice in the decision-making process. Together these entail the right and the obligation of responsible criticism and of reflective consideration of others' criticisms of one's own judgments. Dialogue in which these rights are operative is the essence of the democratic process, a politics of mutuality rather than hostility, and one that encourages and respects individuality rather than reinforcing entrenched "otherness."

NOTES

1. For discussion of Dewey's and Mead's theories of rights, see Joseph Betz's "George Herbert Mead on Human Rights," *Transactions of the Charles S. Peirce Society*, 10, No. 4 (Fall 1974), 199–223, and "John Dewey on Human Rights," ibid., 14, No. 1 (Winter 1978), 18–41.

2. John Dewey, *The Public and Its Problems* (1927), in *John Dewey: The Later Works*. II. *1925–1927*, ed. Jo Ann Boydston (Carbondale and Edwardsville: Southern Illinois University Press, 1988), p. 287; hereafter cited as PP.

3. John Dewey, *Individualism Old and New* (1930), Chapter 4, "The Lost Individual," in *John Dewey: The Later Works*. V. *1929–1930*, ed. Jo Ann Boydston (Carbondale and Edwardsville: Southern Illinois University Press, 1988), p. 67; hereafter cited as ION.

4. ". . . the idea that there is something inherently 'natural' and amenable to natural law, in the working of economic forces . . . is as much a fiction . . . as the doctrine of the individual in possession of antecedent political rights is one in politics" (PP 299). "Dewey's ethics was clearly against Herbert Spencer and worked out along the lines of T. H. Green" (Herbert W. Schneider, "Dewey's Ethics, Part One," in

Guide to the Works of John Dewey, ed. Jo Ann Boydston (Carbondale and Edwardsville: Southern Illinois University Press, 1970, p. 100). Compare Dewey's "The Philosophy of Thomas Hill Green," *Andover Review*, 11 (1889) and "Green's Theory of the Moral Motive," *Philosophical Review* (1892), in *John Dewey: The Early Works*. III. *1889–1892*, ed. Jo Ann Boydston (Carbondale and Edwardsville: Southern Illinois University Press, 1969), pp. 14–35 and 155–173, respectively.

5. John Dewey, *Lectures in China, 1919–1920*, ed. and trans. Robert W. Clopton and Tuin-Chen Ou (Honolulu: The University Press of Hawaii, 1973), p. 151. The English originals have been lost.

6. John Dewey, "Philosophies of Freedom" (1928), in *John Dewey: The Later Works*. III. *1927–1928*, ed. Jo Ann Boydston (Carbondale and Edwardsville: Southern Illinois University Press, 1988), pp. 100–101.

7. John Dewey, *Outlines of a Critical Theory of Ethics* (1891), in *The Early Works*. III. *1889–1892*, ed. Jo Ann Boydston (Carbondale and Edwardsville: Southern Illinois University Press, 1988), p. 348; hereafter cited as CTE.

8. John Dewey and James H. Tufts, *Ethics* (New York: Henry Holt and Co., 1908), p.440. In this first edition of the *Ethics*, Dewey was the author of Part II and the first two chapters of Part III. Part I and the balance of Part III are by Tufts.

9. Ibid., p. 474.

10. Ibid.

11. Ibid., pp. 482–484.

12. John Dewey and James H. Tufts, *Ethics*, 2nd ed. (New York: Henry Holt and Co., 1932), in *John Dewey: The Later Works*. VII. *1932*, ed. Jo Ann Boydston (Carbondale and Edwardsville: Southern Illinois University Press, 1989), pp. 1–462; hereafter cited as 1932 *Ethics*. The Introduction to this edition was jointly written; Dewey is author of Part II (Chapters 10–15) and the first two chapters of Part III (Chapters 16 and 17). It is not clear why the earlier treatment of rights was left out of the 1932 edition.

13. Cf. John J. Stuhr, "Democracy as a Way of Life," in *Philosophy and the Reconstruction of Culture: Pragmatic Essays After Dewey*, ed. John J. Stuhr (Albany: State University of New York Press, 1993), pp. 37–57.

14. John Dewey, "Democracy Is Radical," *Common Sense*, 6 (January 1937), in *John Dewey: The Later Works*. XI. *1935–1937*, ed. Jo Ann Boydston (Carbondale and Edwardsville: Southern Illinois University Press, 1991), p. 297; hereafter cited as DR.

15. John Dewey, "Liberty and Social Control," *Social Frontier*, 2 (November 1935), in *John Dewey: The Later Works*. XI. *1935–1937*, ed. Jo Ann Boydston (Carbondale and Edwardsville: Southern Illinois University Press, 1991), p. 362.

16. John Dewey, *Liberalism and Social Action* (1935), in *John Dewey: The Later Works*. XI. *1935–1937*, ed. Jo Ann Boydston (Carbondale and Edwardsville: Southern Illinois University Press, 1991), p. 63; hereafter cited as LSA.

17. "Democracy and Educational Administration," *Official Report of the Convention of the Department of Superintendence of the National Education Association* (1937), in *John Dewey: The Later Works*. XI. *1935–1937*, ed. Jo Ann Boydston (Carbondale and Edwardsville: Southern Illinois University Press, 1991), pp. 217–218. In the paragraph that follows, Dewey says, "Democratic *political forms* are simply the best means that human wit has devised up to a special time in history. But they rest back upon the idea that no man or limited set of men is wise enough or good enough to rule others without their consent; the positive meaning of this statement is that all those who are affected by social institutions must have a share in producing and managing them" (ibid., p. 218; emphasis added).

18. George Herbert Mead, *Mind, Self, and Society: From the Standpoint of a Social Behaviorist*, ed. Charles W. Morris (Chicago: The University of Chicago Press, 1934); hereafter cited as MSS. "The Psychology of Punitive Justice," *The American Journal of Sociology*, 23 (1917–1918), in *George Herbert Mead: Selected Writings*, ed. Andrew J. Reck (Indianapolis: Bobbs-Merrill, 1964), pp. 212–239; hereafter cited as PJ. "National-Mindedness and International-Mindedness," *International Journal of Ethics*, 39 (1929), in *Selected Writings*, pp. 355–370; hereafter cited as NM. "Natural Rights and the Theory of the Political Institution," *The Journal of Philosophy, Psychology, and Scientific Methods* (1914), in *Selected Writings*, pp. 150–170; hereafter cited as PI.

19. T. H. Green, *Lectures on the Principles of Political Obligation and Other Writings*, ed. Paul Harris and John Morrow (Cambridge: Cambridge University Press, 1968). Cf. Chapter 3 above.

20. Mead speaks of potential universality in connection with the use of significant symbols (whose meaning is defined by the attitude of a generalized other), characterizing this "potential universality" as "an absolute universality for anyone who enters into the language" (MSS 269).

21. George Herbert Mead, *Movements of Thought in the Nineteenth Century*, ed. Merrit H. Moore (Chicago: The University of Chicago Press, 1936), p. 17.

22. Ibid.

23. David Miller, *Market, State, and Community* (Oxford: Clarendon Press, 1989), p. 255; hereafter cited as MSC.

24. Pp. 365. Other than saying that he was a "practical politician," Dewey does not identify Tilden or give the source of his quotation.

Tilden, who had served in the New York State Legislature and served as governor of the state from 1874 to 1876, ran for the presidency of the United States in 1876. He received a quarter-of-a-million–vote plurality in the popular vote but, after the contested electoral votes of four states were awarded to his opponent by a special commission, lost to Rutherford B. Hayes in the Electoral College.

25. Cf. chapters 2 and 4 above.

9

Reconciling Liberalism and Communitarianism

> In debates in the area of political philosophy, we find
> discussions of the proper definition of the public good
> (individualism versus collectivism). Debates in social
> metaphysics moot the possibility of reducing society to
> the individuals which constitute it. . . . To posit a social
> being inevitably suggests a downgrading of the individ-
> ual. Why is this?
>
> —VINCENT DESCOMBES[1]

THE DEBATE BETWEEN INDIVIDUALISM and collectivism in philosophy today is most often formulated as one between liberalism and
communitarianism. What I hope to show in this chapter is that,
on the one hand, society cannot be "reduce[d] . . . to the individuals which constitute it" and, on the other, that valuing community does not necessitate either "a downgrading of the individual"
or a denial of the importance of individual rights. I also hope to
show that placing a high value on individuals and their rights
does not entail sacrificing the common good or the good of the
community. While I see the two issues as related, I will be dealing
with the liberalism/communitarianism controversy from the
point of view of the conflict over individualism rather than that
between the neutralist and communitarian approaches to the issue
concerning conceptions of the good life.

"Liberalism," as John Dewey points out, "has had a checquered
career," and in the United States today we see even more strongly
than in Dewey's day the "inner split" that he saw as having developed between "laissez-faire" liberals and proponents of what we
call the "welfare state."[2] But, at least among political philosophers, the more important split is between liberal individualists
and communitarians. There is considerable variety in each camp,
however, and more and more writers are trying to show that ele-

ments of one are compatible with the other. One such mediator is Amy Gutman, who, in a paper on "Communitarian Critics of Liberalism," asserts that "Communitarianism has the potential for helping us discover a politics that combines community with a commitment to basic liberal values."[3] Another is David Gauthier. Concerning the individualist presuppositions of liberalism, Gauthier, who identifies with liberalism, states, "In defending the normative priority of individual to community we imply nothing about the causal basis of individuality. . . . [I]ndividuality may be socially caused, so that persons are social products. . . ."[4] There is, nevertheless, a conflict between the central commitment of liberalism to individual rights as the main criterion by which to evaluate social policies, and that of comunitarianism to the protection of the community. I see this conflict as resting partly on a particular concept of rights that is shared by proponents of both views, and partly on divergent views of the nature of individual identity. I propose to bridge the gap between the two approaches by providing analyses of identity and of rights that show both to be inseparable from community. I shall also argue that communities as well as individuals can and should have rights, and that there is no necessary or inherent conflict between the two. Those conflicts that arise, like conflicts between individual rights themselves, are circumstantial.

Contrasting certain features of Adam Smith's economic liberalism with the contractarian liberalism it succeeded, Dewey notes that "[t]he concern for liberty and for the individual, which was the basis of Lockeian liberalism, persisted; otherwise the newer theory would not have been liberalism" (LSA 9). And, as he reminds us, "The outstanding points of Locke's version of liberalism are that governments are instituted to protect the rights that belong to individuals prior to political organization of social relations" (LSA 6–7). In most of its versions, the contemporary liberal ideal of justice retains this notion of antecedent rights and, as Michael Sandel notes, embodies the claim "that individual rights cannot be sacrificed for the sake of the common good."[5] Challenging the liberal view (and both traditional rationalist and empiricist concepts of the self), communitarians deny the assumption underlying the concept of antecedent rights, namely, that personal identity is independent of membership in society. Instead, they

see personal liberty as largely a function of membership in a community and, consequently, give moral as well as metaphysical priority to communities. In an important paper on "Atomism," the
name he gives to the individualism of the contractarian tradition,
Charles Taylor uses the communitarian theory of identity to turn
the liberal concept of the priority of individual rights against itself:
"[T]he free individual, the bearer of rights," he says, "can only
assume this identity thanks to his relationship to a developed liberal civilization; . . . there is an absurdity in placing this subject in
a state of nature where he could never attain this identity and
hence never create by contract a society which respects it." Because this is the case, Taylor holds, "the free individual who affirms himself as such *already* has an obligation to complete, restore,
or sustain the society within which this identity is possible."[6]
Nevertheless, as I shall show, Alasdair MacIntyre and other communitarian thinkers presuppose the traditional view of rights as
belonging to individuals independently of their affiliation with
any community and base their negative evaluation of individual
rights upon this assumption.

The assertion of universal, individual human rights is often accompanied by a denial that groups or communities can or ought
to have rights. Sometimes this is based on the metaphysical premise that groups are not real, that they are reducible to their individual members.[7] To accommodate this and to deal with them as
if they had rights, corporations and other collectivities are treated,
in American legal practice, as "artificial persons." Not surprisingly, this individualism with regard to rights tends to be associated with the atomistic, presocial view of the self that Taylor
criticizes. Sandel, in attributing it to John Rawls, refers to this as
the concept of "the unencumbered self" (US 14). On this view,
all humans are assumed to be independent possessors of the same
universal human nature, and today's liberal version of "natural
rights," like its predecessors, holds rights to be inherent traits of
all beings who share in it.[8] Developing their views in the struggles
against oppressive governments, thinkers such as Locke and
Thomas Jefferson further conceived rights in adversarial terms as
being held by individuals against governments; their intellectual
descendants construe them as being held against one another or
against society. As Loren Lomasky puts it, to talk about rights

is to talk about "the justified claims of individuals against their governments and against each other."[9] Seemingly taking this individualist and adversarial concept of rights to be the only one, communitarians, if they do not reject the principle of individual rights altogether, at least argue that rights should be subordinated to the collective goals of traditional or cultural communities and to policies designed for their survival. Identifying "human rights" with "natural rights"—"rights attaching to human beings simply *qua* human beings"—Alasdair MacIntyre denies them, contending that "such rights . . . are fictions."[10] Taylor, whom we can class as a moderate communitarian despite his expressed discomfort with the label,[11] points out, regarding the Canadian Charter of Rights and Freedoms of 1982,

> The new patriotism of the Charter has given an impetus to a philosophy of rights and of non-discrimination that is highly suspicious of collective goals. It can only countenance them if they are clearly subordinated to individual rights and to provisions of non-discrimination. But for those who take these goals seriously, this subordination is unacceptable.[12]

There is a direct relation between the different attitudes toward individual rights held by liberals and communitarians and their different ways of conceiving personal identity and moral agency. For the modern liberal, the rights-holder is an independent actor, unconditioned by social status or cultural identity. As the sociologist Zygmunt Bauman points out, the framework of law in Western, modern, capitalist society "names the individual human being as the subject of rights, obligations and responsibilities; . . . [it] holds the individual, and the individual alone, responsible for his or her actions; . . . [it] defines the action as a kind of behavior which has the intention of the actor as its ultimate cause and explanation . . . [and] explains what has happened by the purpose the actor set for himself." The practices that follow from this individualism, he notes, reinforce our commonsense belief that this is the case.[13] Speaking of this idea of the self as moral agent, MacIntyre characterizes it as that of a "democratised self which has no necessary social content and no necessary social identity" and which "can then be anything, can assume any role or take any point of view, because it *is* in and for itself nothing" (AV 30).

It would seem that, in the context of liberal thought, the atomic individual is reduced to a cipher.

Developing his own concept of "narrative identity," MacIntyre says, first, that "personal identity is just that identity presupposed by the unity of the character which the unity of a narrative [which runs from one's birth to one's death] requires." But this is only one dimension of identity; MacIntyre goes on to point out that there are others who enter into the narrative, and "I am part of their story, as they are part of mine" (AV 203).[14] "[W]e all approach our own circumstances," he says, "as bearers of a particular social identity" (AV 205). Taylor construes this social identity in terms of individuals' conscious identification with what sociologists call a "reference group"; it is their self-definition as members of the group or community and their sense of this shared identity. Writing on the "politics of recognition," Taylor notes that the term "identity," in this context, "designates something like a person's understanding of who they are, of their fundamental characteristics as a human being."[15] The reference is not to universal human characteristics; "identity" here refers to the characteristics in terms of which one identifies with the other members of a cultural group or segment of society (such as women) to which one belongs, and as a member of which one identifies oneself, that is, one's sense of identity or belonging. But "identity," for him, connotes more than this. In an article on nationalism, Taylor puts it this way:

> The conception of identity is the view that outside the horizon provided by some master value or some allegiance or some community membership, I would be crucially crippled, . . . unable to function as a fully human subject. . . . The horizon necessary for me is not essential for human beings as such. . . . [T]he claim about identity is particularized. I may come to realize that belonging to a given culture is part of my identity because outside of the reference points of this culture I could not begin to put to myself, let alone answer, those questions of ultimate significance that are peculiarly in the repertory of the human subject. So this culture helps to identify me.[16]

Individual identity thus encompasses cultural identity. Equally important, Taylor takes identity, whether that of an individual, a group, or a society, to be the product of dialogue. Using "language" in the broadest possible sense to include all modes of expression, he says, in "The Politics of Recognition," "People do not acquire the languages needed for self-definition on their own. Rather, we are introduced to them through interaction with others . . ." (PRec 32). Personal identity is, therefore, social in origin as well as content.[17] And included in the social content is the "conception of the good life" proper to that person's cultural community, the "definition of the good actually embedded in [its] practices" (DV 76).

I agree with Taylor regarding the largely social nature and origin of personal identity. And, using the term 'perspective' in a sense that is roughly equivalent to Taylor's—and Gadamer's—"horizon," I construe this identity in terms of the perspectives that individuals acquire, most of them, I agree, in dialogic interaction with others. I also agree with Taylor that the values embedded in a culture are important constituents of individual as well as cultural identity. But when I speak of identity I do not refer to individual or collective self-identification or to the sense of identity. Rather, by personal identity, I mean the identifiable character of the individual self as it is manifest in the behavior and judgments that emanate from and reflect that person's perspective. Not only is an individual's perspective largely shaped and conditioned by the culture of a society; it is analogous to such a culture. But we must remember that the individual is a member of indefinitely many communities of other sorts in addition to a cultural (or ethnic) community, and the perspectives of these communities are also constituents of individual identity. (Here, as elsewhere, I am using the term 'community' as a name for the genus of which groups, families, and societies—human collectivities of all sorts—are species.) If only because these differ from one person to another, even within a cultural community, I think we must attach greater significance to individuality than the communitarians seem to; in my view those features of an individual's character or perspective that are shared are constituents of an identity that is irreducibly individual.

Part of the importance of the concept of perspective is that it is through sharing perspectives that individuals are enabled to communicate with one another. And it is through shared normative perspectives, systems of social norms operative among them, that persons regulate their interpersonal and intercommunal relations. Only because of this sharing can either individuals or communities have rights. I claim that both can do so and, in addition, that persons can have rights collectively that they cannot have as individuals but that differ from the rights of communities as such. All three—individual rights, collective rights, and communal rights—play a role in human social existence; none precludes either of the others; and none is inherently more or less significant. Determinations regarding relative importance in particular situational contexts are decisions that must be arrived at by the persons and communities involved.

IDENTITY AND COMMUNITY

What I hope to do in what follows is to show in somewhat greater detail how individuality and community are related and demonstrate the consequences of this for rights and, hence, for the liberalism/communitarianism debate. Some of what I say will repeat what has been said in the previous section or in earlier parts of this book but is included in the interest of clarity. And in some cases, what will be said is an elaboration or amendment of an earlier statement.

A community in the broadest sense is a number of people (at least two) who share a common perspective, that is, who have the same attitude toward or way of responding to some thing or complex, whatever it may be. A good example of this is the community of all those who love babies. While it may seem trivial, community in this minimal sense is the first prerequisite of communication. Just imagine two people from utterly different cultures and speaking mutually incomprehensible languages watching a baby and exchanging smiles. The sort of community in which rights are operative, of course, is quite different from this merely perspectival community. It is what I call a 'normative community'. This is a community whose unifying perspective is a set of social norms, principles or rules that are developed in the attempt to coordinate behavior and facilitate higher-level communication and that serve as standards or prescriptions for behavior and practice. An example of such a community, although it is not an organized one, is the nearly worldwide community of those who understand and know we should obey the international road signs. This understanding is a shared normative perspective. In an organized community such as a team, a business firm, or an educational institution, all members or potential members are explicitly required to internalize the norms (or to have already done so) and, without good reasons for not doing so in particular circumstances, to govern themselves by them. But the expectation that its norms are operative among its members is an ingredient in the perspective of any normative community. An important feature of this expectation is that it is mutual: the nature of social norms is such that anyone who has internalized them not only expects all the others who are assumed to belong to the community to take the norms into account in determining how to behave, but also understands that she or he, too, is expected to do so.

Whether through purely personal experience or in interaction with others, every human being develops a characteristic personal perspective or general attitude: a complex of perspectives that condition the way she or he responds to particular things or situations. Among the constituent perspectives are some that are private or idiosyncratic. But many are shared and, of these, the most important are the normative perspectives that govern all but the most rudimentary social conduct, interaction, and communication. A personal perspective is complex, but its constituents are interrelated, even though not every one is related to every other; and even though many (or most) of its components are common to many persons, the fact that it is a unique constellation of perspectives distinguishes every personal perspective from all others. Moreover, while most of its constituents change, continuities and relations among them persist, as do memories, so that despite their differences, one's perspective as a small child and one's perspective as an adult belong to the same person. Shaping the way one behaves, responds, thinks, reasons, one's perspective determines—in a significant sense it *is*—one's character or identity as that particular individual. And in virtue of the continuities from one stage to another, one's identity at any point in one's development is part of one's identity as the same developing and changing individual.

The common perspective that unites diverse persons in any given community joins individuals whose personal perspectives differ in other respects. They share only selected perspectives, and each shared perspective is itself that of another community. Now consider a self-conscious individual—yourself, for instance. The continuities among your diverse perspectives are comparable to the shared perspectives of different individuals. For example, you may view one and the same child both as your offspring and as a potential citizen, the two perspectives connected by your recognition of the youngster *as* a child. Each of these causes you to treat that child in distinctive ways, and your personal perspective encompasses both. As shared perspectives enable different individuals—members of that perspectival community—to communicate with one another, relations among your own perspectives enable you to communicate with yourself. At any given time you have or can adopt a perspective in the light of which to consider some element of your experience or memory, some idea or feeling to which that perspective is relevant; alternatively, you can shift from one perspective on the same complex to another or apply that same perspective to other things; *and* you can adopt or devise a perspective in which to compare the ways different things appear or the way the same thing appears in the different perspectives, as well as one that enables you to analyze, compare, or criticize those perspectives themselves. This is to say that you, too, have the defining trait of a community: a general perspective in which diverse perspectives intersect and which, by allowing you to adopt now one and now another of these, enables you to communicate, reflexively, with yourself. Thus, in addition to belonging to innumerable social communities, in an important sense, every human individual *is* a community—what Justus Buchler terms a "reflexive community."[18] Not only are community and individuality inseparable, but the identity of each is a function of the perspectival complex that conditions its behavior and thereby gives the person or the community its distinct, identifiable character. At the same time, just as the perspective of any community enters into and helps to shape the perspectives of its members, the perspective of a normative community is a product of their communicative interaction. The community, that is, is not reducible to its members but is at one and the same time their creation and a condition of their personal identity.

RIGHTS

That all humans are endowed with inalienable rights, either by a Creator God or because these rights are inherent in what it means to be human, is an ideal, not a statement of fact. Potent as this ideal may be, even if there are innate rights to life, liberty, and the pursuit of happiness, they are inoperative for large segments of humanity, and it is hard to see what it means for those persons to "have" them. Even if we are assumed to have "natural" or God-given rights, we need to understand what it means for them to be operative, and in developing my own view, when I speak of rights I always mean *operative* rights.[19] But in either sense of the term, as the British philosopher Margaret MacDonald has pointed out, rights cannot be "endowments" or traits of human individuals or of human nature since they are prescriptive. To say someone "has" a right is not to describe a particular characteristic of that person or of human beings in general, but to say that others ought to behave in a certain way toward him or her.[20] Rights, that is, are principles that can and ought to govern human conduct; where they are operative, these principles are established as social norms.

That this is a function of norms rather than of laws is an important stipulation, because there can be rights that are respected even though they are not written into law and rights that are prescribed by law but are not operative. Like all social norms, rights-norms exist and are operative in communities and in the conjoined lives of their members; they are elements in the normative perspective shared by those individuals. That is, no right can actually exist without being operative in some community: it must be acknowledged, whether explicitly or implicitly. For there to be universal human rights would be for there to be a universal normative community with established and operative rights-norms. While we can hope that there may someday be one, and work for the realization of this ideal, it has yet to be actualized and may never be so.

As operative social norms, rights are social institutions. I am not the first or the only philosopher to see them in this way. As Rex Martin puts it, "a right is an established way of acting," and "for there to be rights (for [these] ways of acting to be established) norms must be formulated. . . ."[21] But what would these norms prescribe? Rights have been variously described. Hohfeld, upon whose work many contemporary rights theorists draw, identifies four categories of rights: liberties, powers, immunities, and claims.[22] Others limit rights to one or more of these. But to be rights, liberties, powers, and immunities must be conferred, and respect for them required, by a community; and while we may claim rights, claims per se, even those we find to be valid or justi-fied, are not rights unless they are established as such in and by a community.

With Virginia Held, I take rights to be entitlements, entitle-ments to act in certain ways or to have or receive specified things. But I do not define them, as she does, simply as entitlements yielded by valid rules or principles, even though such rules and principles might prompt the conclusion that there ought to be certain rights.[23] Valid rules or principles do not themselves yield or give rise to operative rights; these require the establishment of social norms that prescribe the kind of behavior that rights entail. To be an entitlement that one has *by right* requires, moreover, that anyone in a position to do so be empowered to claim it and, second, that respect for it be obligatory, so that we can be com-pelled to enforce it. The first stipulation is what distinguishes a right from a privilege, a right being granted to all to whom it might ever apply, with no one antecedently excluded. (Since rights are operative among the members of a community, we must presuppose that they can apply only within the community. I shall discuss this issue subsequently.) Regarding the second point, if respect for it were not obligatory, mandated by the norms, an entitlement would not have the force of a right; the obligation to respect it is an intrinsic component of the right, correlative to and conferred jointly with the entitlement. While we speak of entitlements themselves as rights, technically, a right is a relation between the entitlement and the obligation—in practice, a relation between or among those in a position to exercise the entitlement and those in a position to show respect for it. Most important in the present context, since rights-entitlements and the obligation to respect them are correlative and inseparable, and since both are conferred upon every member of the community in which rights are operative, rights are mutual rather than adversarial relations among rights-holders. As such, individual rights are no threat to social cohesion. On the contrary, they promote it.

Not all entitlements, even those protected by social policy or law, are rights. However well justified, protected entitlements granted to selected subjects—such as the sort of "special rights" Will Kymlicka and others would grant to certain minorities— even if they are established and enforceable by law, are privileges, not rights.[24] Rights and privileges are often confused: Taylor, for instance, speaks of rights as "privileges that are seen to belong to subjects" (NS 47). But privileges are the opposite of rights, and, as institutions, rights "belong" to the communities in which they are established as much as to the individuals who thereby participate in them.

RIGHTS-BEARERS

Who can and should have rights? To begin with, to actually have a right is at least to be a member of a community in which rights-norms are operative. Second, as I have defined it, a right has two reciprocal and inseparable components: a specified entitlement and an obligation to respect that entitlement, both conferred by the social norms. Thus, to have rights, to participate in this social institution, presupposes the ability not only to understand what it is to have an entitlement and to respect entitlements, but also to acknowledge the obligation to do so and hold others to be similarly obligated. Nonhuman animals, then, cannot have rights. And while infants must be treated as if they participate in this institution in order for them to learn what it means and to internalize the norms governing it, those who would ordinarily be expected to have these abilities but cannot develop them, or who have lost the capacity to govern themselves by the norms, must either be granted comparable benefits or participate in the social relations involved in rights through being represented by others.

There is nothing in the nature or structure of rights that inherently limits rights to individuals. Communities, like individuals, can belong to more inclusive communities, and the norms of an inclusive community can include rights-norms, not only those applicable to individuals but norms that confer rights-entitlements on member communities. An example would be the right of religious organizations to exist in a community, free of discrimination and prejudice. As a right, this entitlement would have to be granted to all such organizations and is one that not only they, but all individuals and communities that are part of the wider community and thus bound by its norms, would be obligated to respect.

But for communities as such, as distinguished from their members, to exercise rights-entitlements and express respect for them, they must be able to act *as* communities, to function as unitary entities. Take, as an example, the right of each of the member states of the United Nations to have a say in the decisions of that body. This right can be implemented only because there is a mechanism enabling each state to act: each has a designated representative with the power to act in its name. Representation is not the only such mechanism. An act of Congress is an act of that body as a whole in virtue of the voting procedure and the principle of majority rule. There are other rights, however, that are exercised, not by communities as entities, but by their members jointly or collectively. Such a right would be the right of an ethnic or cultural community to pursue its own way of life. This right can be exercised only by its members jointly participating in their characteristic norm-governed practices—holding their traditional religious services, communicating with one another in their own language, and so on—and keeping those ways alive. The term 'collective rights', employed by some philosophers for all community rights, is more properly applied to those that are exercised by individuals collectively, and this is the way I use it. For the rights of communities as such, I use the name 'communal rights'. The category of 'community rights' includes both. But for either communal or collective rights to be operative, they must be established within a wider community whose norms mandate respect for them by all its subcommunities and all their members, individually and collectively. The inclusive community itself may or may not share in a given rights-entitlement, but as the agent or representative of all its member communities, it must implement the obligation to respect it and, where necessary, take steps to enforce it. States' rights, for example, are not applicable to the United States as a whole, but the national government must see to it that they are respected. But consider the right to levy taxes, which, in the United States, is applicable to communities at several levels: the nation itself, the states that are subcommunities within it, the counties within the states, the cities and towns within the counties—all have the entitlement and all are obligated to respect one another's entitlement. Insofar as they do, this right is not merely legal, but is an operative right, an accepted social norm that is implemented in practice. However, in relation to the individuals (or organizations) who must pay taxes, the right to levy them must be classified as a power; individuals do not participate in the communal right.

FUNDAMENTAL RIGHTS

If rights are not features of universal human nature, are there rights that *ought to be* universal? An answer in the affirmative would seem to mean that there should be universally operative rights-norms. But while it would seem that common features of the human condition unite all humankind in a universal perspectival community, the possibility of a universal community of rights or, more generally, a universal normative community, is remote. However, I maintain that there are rights that ought to be *generic*, i.e., operative for all human beings in the sense of being operative in all normative communities. (For convenience, I speak of these *as* generic rights.) And I also argue that comparable rights ought to be operative for all communities.

While there is no universal normative community, there is no human being who does not belong to innumerable particular communities in which norms are operative. I contend that there are two rights that, because of the nature and the importance of normative community, ought to be operative in every one. In addition to these two *fundamental* generic rights, I have identified a number of others that, because they are either presupposed by any exercise of the fundamental rights or entailed by them, should also be generic. These include rights such as those that entitle individuals to nutrition and health care, to education, to economic opportunity—access to the means of support—and the right of all to be treated as equals. Some of these can be implemented only in certain kinds of community: linguistic communities, such as the community of all speakers of English, cannot provide nutrition or health care. For such rights to be operative for all humans, the norms that govern them would have to be established in, and govern the relevant policies and institutions of, every community in which the entitlements involved can be satisfied.[25]

What are the fundamental generic rights and how are they justified? Human beings are distinguished from other animals in that humans cannot exist without culture in the broad sense, that is, without systems of interrelated social norms. I do not deny that rudimentary norms can and do evolve among groups of nonhuman animals, but an enduring system or structure of norms is not a precondition of the existence of an animal herd or band. There is no analogy among other animal species to the diverse normative communities that prevail among humans. But normative community is the necessary prerequisite of a distinctively human existence. The different societies that humans have evolved, the kind of communities with which communitarians such as MacIntyre and Taylor are concerned, and to which the term 'culture' is commonly confined, are normative communities and each encompasses a variety of normative subcommunities.

Norms evolve and come to be accepted in the course of joint purposive activity, as ways of organizing or directing that activity, whatever it may be. Passed on from generation to generation, operative norms may be consciously and deliberately maintained or revised. But they may also come to be habitual and can be perpetuated—or lapse into disuse and lose their normative force—unquestioningly and even without anyone's noticing or calling attention to this. We are ordinarily unaware of many, if not most, of the norms to which we nevertheless conform. But conditions and circumstances change, calling for changes in our accepted ways of doing things and the norms that these express. As Dewey says, when action is blocked, we have to reflect. We do not always do so in a methodic way, but the more deliberately and critically we reflect and consider what we ought to do and how, the more carefully we test the ways and means that seem to promise the results that we desire, the more likely it is that the new guidelines that emerge will prove satisfactory and will come to be accepted as normative. The more central the activity or institution is to our lives, the more important is this process of reconstructing the norms that govern it, and the more important it is that we all bring to it our powers of reflection, analysis, prediction, and critical evaluation. Think of the problems we are encountering today in the sphere of the family, where accepted norms seem to have lost their force and new principles have yet to win social acceptance.

As we reinforce or reconstruct the norms of any community, we perpetuate or reshape its characteristic culture, the shared perspective that George Herbert Mead calls "the attitude of the generalized other."[26] The material culture—the technology and the artifacts that may also characterize the community—both affects and is affected by changes in the norms. And as we shape and reshape the culture, we are helping to shape the character and attitude of those who internalize and live by its norms—the personal perspectives of the community's members. The more widespread and pervasive the activities that they govern, the greater the role specific norms play in determining the social dimension of individual identity. For all these reasons—the indispensability of a normative structure, the ubiquity of normative breakdown and the need for revision, and the import of norms for both individual and community identity—we should consider the norms of the communities to which we belong to be always open to critical assessment and subject to change. There is another reason as well, analogous to the epistemological fallibilism adopted by Charles S. Peirce and other pragmatist philosophers, who hold that no judgment should ever be taken to be incorrigible. Praxical or practical fallibilism would hold that we can never be absolutely certain that our way of doing anything will not, in some situation, turn out to be inadequate or that it could not be improved upon.

On all these grounds, I would argue, *first*, that every member of every normative community should be entitled to participate in the determination, criticism, and revision of its norms—to participate on an equal footing with all the other members in whatever interaction or dialogue is involved in this process; and, *second*, that, as a participant, each should be entitled to exercise his or her own powers of judgment. To put this in the more formal language I have employed: every member of every actual or potential normative community should be accorded two rights, which I take to be the fundamental generic rights. These are a right of *personal authority* and a right of *personal autonomy*. Every member of the community who has the capacity to do so should be accepted as a legitimate and worthy participant in shaping the social norms and, in the course of these determinations, should be entitled to arrive at and put forth his or her own judgments. As with all rights, for each of these to be operative presupposes that every participant accord the same entitlement to all the others. The right of authority mandates that the judgments of each be taken seriously by the others, which means that the participants must be not only self-critical but also open to one another's criticisms. It may seem surprising that I say these rights should be accorded in every "potential" as well as "actual" normative community; but this is both possible and necessary because the very establishment of these (or any) rights among individuals who have not previously been united in a normative community serves so to unite them and to create such a community.

Authority is to be taken here, not as any power to command obedience, or in the sense of expertise, but in a sense closer to (though not synonymous with) authoritativeness. The right of authority is the entitlement to respectful attention, to be taken seriously as a presumptively competent participant in dialogic interaction. Autonomy, even more than other technical terms, has been used in diverse ways. The typical dictionary definition is self-government or self-determination. It has also been construed in Hobbesian fashion as liberty, in the negative sense of freedom from external constraints (presupposing the power of voluntary action). John Rawls states that "persons are acting autonomously [when] they are acting from principles that they would acknowledge under conditions that best express their nature as free and equal rational beings."[27] Rawls rests his concept on the Kantian view of autonomy, of the individual as an independent, inherently rational, moral legislator, prescribing universal moral laws *a priori* and without regard for social or situational conditions. Autonomy has also been construed to mean living as a free person, having "an autonomous life," as Joseph Raz puts it.[28] He takes the essence of such a life to be the exercise of "free or deliberate choice of options" as "opposed to a life of coerced choices." This is not simply a life of Hobbesian liberty but "an ideal of self-creation."[29] When I prescribe a right of personal autonomy, I do not mean any of these, although my concept incorporates elements of most of them. What I mean by autonomy can be said to be self-determination in a particular sense, namely, the exercise of one's own judgment: one's power to consider, reflect, reason, evaluate, take positions, arrive at decisions and act upon them, as well as assert and argue for one's judgments, and to reconsider them.[30] But an autonomous judgment, like an autonomous action, is not simply voluntary or self-determined. One may voluntarily submit to coercion (say, to avoid punishment), but an autonomous judgment is one that is not arrived at under coercion. At the same time, even autonomous judgment is not free of all constraints. All but the most rudimentary judgment presupposes and is conditioned by norms, those governing language and reasoning, for example; and dialogue with others presupposes, and may generate, additional norms governing the treatment of the subject at hand and the interaction of the participants.

In addition, we cannot judge without having or adopting a position or perspective toward whatever it is we are considering. Nevertheless, as creatures capable of reflection we can be critical and self-critical. We can adopt or devise perspectives by which to judge other judgments and other perspectives, including our own, and including those normative perspectives in terms of which we determine our own behavior. It is respect for the autonomy of persons understood to be capable of this kind of judgment (that is, all ordinary adults and even youngsters who show what we take to be "good judgment") that, I contend, ought to be exercised wherever and whenever the members of a community must determine the ways in which their life together is to be conducted. The fact that we are continually revising our practices and

our shared assumptions implies that the right of autonomy, together with that of authority, should be operative in all the affairs
of every normative community.

Having argued that the rights of autonomy and authority
should be conferred on all individual members of all normative
communities, I argue as well that there should also be analogous
communal and collective rights. Let me briefly indicate the
grounds for this contention. To begin with, communities that
interact with one another need to develop ways of regulating
their mutual relations. That is, they must develop social norms
that will be operative among them, institutionalized in the inclusive communities to which they belong and understood to be
binding on all the member communities. Unlike those governing
individual behavior, such norms almost always have to be explicitly formulated. Second, the same requirement of voluntary acceptance holds for the norms that are to govern communities as
holds for those relevant to individuals; if social norms are to be
operative among communities, they must be jointly instituted (or
modified) and collectively perpetuated by those communities.
And, as with norms governing individual behavior, legislation is
not sufficient unless the laws and regulations that are passed are
taken to be binding and put into practice.

The right of communal authority is the entitlement of every
community engaged in interaction with others (thus joined with
them in a more inclusive community) to have a voice in determining the way their joint activities and interactions are to be
governed—i.e., in determining the norms by which these are to
be regulated—and to be accorded respect as a participant on an
equal footing with all the others. Like that of personal autonomy,
the concept of autonomy as it applies to communities needs clarification. It is not to be construed here as sovereignty or political
independence. In the case of a political community or state, it
does entail self-government in a political sense; but in the more
general sense that I intend, it is analogous to personal autonomy.
For a community to be autonomous is, first of all, for its members,
collectively and without coercion, to determine and govern
themselves by their own social norms. This is what I mean by
collective autonomy, and the members of every (normative) community should have a collective right to autonomy in this sense.

Communal autonomy, that of a community as an entity, presupposes that the community has the ability to act as a body, which means, as noted earlier, that it has mechanisms whereby it can arrive at decisions and make commitments that are representative of it as an entity. That is, the community must have agential power, the power of self-determination. To exercise this power autonomously is to do so in the absence of external or internal coercion. (For any faction or subcommunity within the community to enforce its will in determining how that community is to act would be a case of internal coercion and would limit both the communal autonomy of the community and the collective autonomy of the rest of its members.) The right of communal autonomy, then, is the entitlement, extended by mutually accepted norms, to every agential community within an inclusive community, to exercise its power of self-determination without coercion. It is applicable to all the relations of the subcommunities to one another, but is especially important in connection with the shaping and reshaping of the norms by which their mutual interactions and relations are to be governed. In the end, both collective and communal autonomy rest on the input of the individual members of the communities involved, who should have comparable rights of autonomy and authority. But, in turn, these rights can be made operative only by the development, within each community, of norms defining them as such.

IMPLICATIONS

Contrary to the fears of communitarians, individual rights do not endanger the stability or integrity of communities. To begin with, both personal identity and individual rights are inseparably linked to membership in communities. Individuality and community are mutually constitutive, and the generation of social norms by persons in community with one another is the precondition and the source of all the rights that are actually operative in society. Furthermore, being reciprocal—consisting in mutually recognized entitlements and obligations to respect them—rights are not adversarial. They do not divide people from one another nor do they set them against governments or states. While there can be situations in which one's rights-entitlements are threatened or violated and it may be necessary to defend them, to claim or exercise an entitlement on the ground that it is a right is not to pit oneself against others; it is to say that they ought to respect it exactly as one does oneself and would also do were they to assert it. Nor are individual rights held against the community, even though the community or, in the case of a civic community, its government, can be called upon to protect them and to punish violators. Even political rights such as the right to vote, insofar as they are acknowledged and respected by the citizens—i.e., insofar as they are operative, rather than merely legislated—are entitlements defined (together with the correlative obligation to respect them) by the norms. This is to say that they are accorded by the citizens to one another, each standing both in the position of the community itself (as having the attitude of the generalized other) and in that of a member of that community. The function of government in relation to individual rights is an instrumental one. In the first place, it can have powers of adjudication as well as of enforcement delegated to it. In exercising the power to protect operative rights and to adjudicate conflicts involving those rights, a government or governmental agency is acting for the citizens themselves, individually and collectively. And, having the power to enact laws, it can also codify operative rights-norms, again performing an instrumental function and serving the community.

Beyond this, government can legislate that certain rights are to be the law of the land; but the enactment of such laws is not sufficient of itself to make those rights operative among the citizens, and enforcing them is not guaranteed to do so either. Even a government that is formally a democratic, representative one acting in the name of the citizens may pass legislation, including legislation establishing rights, that does not express, or even runs counter to, the norms and values of the community. But even were this not the case, neither the power of legislation nor any others among the legitimate powers of government over individual conduct are properly understood as rights against the citizens. They are not rights because they are not reciprocal; the citizens have no comparable entitlements or powers. And if they were rights, they would, by definition, be mutual, not adversarial, and so would not be held "against" anyone. Communities can have rights, however. The rights that are operative for them are actually supported by the exercise of the individual rights of autonomy and authority, since for communal or collective rights to be operative, they must be so within an inclusive community, which requires that they be respected not only by all its subcommunities, but also by their individual members.

At least in principle, then, individual and community rights are compatible. However, we cannot ignore the fact that particular rights, whether those of communities or those of individuals, may come into conflict with one another, and it may happen that one and the same entitlement cannot be exercised by two parties at once. It is for this reason that rights cannot be taken to be absolute. Even when government steps in, definitive and lasting resolution of such conflicts—solutions which all the claimants not only accept but will be willing to abide by—are more likely to be achieved with the autonomous and authoritative participation of those concerned—the exercise of what I have termed 'dialogic reciprocity'. It may be that a given right, whether in virtue of its content or because of social or cultural conditions, repeatedly or even inevitably conflicts with other rights that are considered important. Such a problematic right calls for change, again with the autonomous and authoritative participation of as many members of the community as possible. This applies whether the conflict is within a community of persons or between or among communities within a more inclusive community. But another sort of possible conflict is that between rights operative for individuals and those operative for communities, and it might be asked whether this does not have implications for the liberalism/communitarianism controversy. Should community rights take precedence over individual rights or vice versa? Are conflicts between them inherently conflicts between individual interests and the good of the community?

One problematic example of such a conflict is that which has occasionally arisen between the right to freedom of speech and expression operative for individuals in democratic countries and the right, also operative therein, of religious communities to perpetuate traditional practices and rules that prohibit—or are construed by some to prohibit—certain forms of free expression on the part of their members (who are also members of the wider community). But these conflicts relate to particular norms and practices, and are products of specific conditions. Nothing in the nature of either community or personal identity, and nothing in the nature of rights, necessitates that communal and individual rights must conflict with one another. And, whether in dealing with particular cases or in shaping the norms of society, there is nothing that determines *a priori* or universally whether the interests of communities or those of their individual members or subcommunities should be accorded greater weight. But conflicts of the sort mentioned, like any conflicts of rights or of social norms in general, call for open and public discussion in which the personal rights of autonomy and authority are respected equally with those of the communities involved. While there is no guarantee that every conflict will be satisfactorily resolved, rational consideration of the sort that Dewey identifies with the method of democracy makes a workable solution more likely.[31] And, even if they pose a threat to the integrity of a community, conflicts can also be stimuli to social change, to the modification or alteration of the relevant norms, and even, in this way, to enhancing the solidarity of a community.

Two further points are in order. The main concern of communitarians is with cultural communities in the narrow sense of this term: communities with their own languages and ways of life. The right to communal autonomy, for such a community, is its right to its own culture, a right that would also be a collective right for the community's members. But, regarding every normative community, cultural communities not excepted, we must recognize that the exercise of autonomy and authority by its members may result in change. To affirm the fundamental individual rights of the members of a cultural community as well as their collective right to perpetuate their own social institutions is to accept this possibility, even as it is to affirm the community's right to its own way of life. As with individual identity, it is continuity rather than sameness that marks the identity of a community or a culture over time; and while we can argue for the value of cultural traditions, languages, and ideals and for the importance of preserving them, this is not the same as making their survival an end in itself. To do so—as, for instance, Quebec's Bill 101 (discussed by Taylor) does in requiring French-speaking parents to send their children to those schools in which French, not English, is the language of instruction in order to ensure that French culture is perpetuated—would be to violate their collective as well as their personal autonomy in a way that simply ensuring the availability of such schools would not.[32] In addition, cultural communities are not the only ones for which rights can and ought to be operative. To take but a single example: it is essential for political groups and organizations, which are also normative communities in the sense intended here, to have and to respect the fundamental rights of autonomy and authority—that is, the right of each to develop and express its own positions on issues and to be given a respectful hearing, and equally respectful criticism, in the public arena. (The corollary to this, of course, is the mutual obligation to discuss all such criticism seriously before deciding whether to accept or reject it.) It is equally important for the members of these groups to participate in the same fundamental rights within them as well as in the community at large. Together, these are the rights I take to be definitive of democracy; all ought to be established in every political community and subcommunity and protected by government and by the citizens.

NOTES

1. Vincent Descombes, "Is There an Objective Spirit?" in *Philosophy in an Age of Pluralism: The Philosophy of Charles Taylor in Question*, ed. James Tully (Cambridge: Cambridge University Press, 1994), p. 100.

2. John Dewey, *Liberalism and Social Action* (1935), in *John Dewey: The Later Works. XI. 1935–1937*, ed. Jo Ann Boydston (Carbondale and Edwardsville: Southern Illinois University Press, 1991), pp. 1–65; hereafter cited as LSA.

3. Amy Gutman, "Communitarian Critics of Liberalism," *Philosophy and Public Affairs*, 14, No. 3 (Summer 1985), repr. in *Communitarianism and Individualism*, ed. Shlomo Avineri and Avner de Shalit (Oxford: Oxford University Press, 1992), p. 133.

4. David Gauthier, "The Liberal Individual," excerpts from *Morals by Agreement* (Oxford: Oxford University Press, 1986), repr. in ibid., p. 157.

5. Michael Sandel, "The Procedural Republic and the Unencumbered Self," *Political Theory*, 12 (1984), repr. in *Communitarianism and*

Individualism, ed. Shlomo Avineri and Avner de Shalit (Oxford: Oxford University Press, 1992), p.13; hereafter cited as US.

6. Charles Taylor, "Atomism," in *Powers, Possessions, and Freedom*, ed. Alkis Kontos (Toronto: University of Toronto Press, 1979); excerpt reprinted in *Communitarianism and Individualism*, ed. Avineri and de Shalit, p. 49.

7. Cf. Lon Fuller, *Legal Fictions* (Stanford, California: Stanford University Press, 1967).

8. Cf. A. P. d'Entrèves, "A Theory of Natural Rights," in *Natural Law: An Historical Survey* (London: Hutchinson University Library, 1951; repr. New York: Harper Torchbooks, 1965).

9. Loren Lomasky, *Persons, Rights, and the Moral Community* (New York: Oxford University Press, 1987), p. 11. The classic statement of this adversarial concept of rights as claims against others is Wesley N. Hohfeld's in *Fundamental Legal Conceptions*, ed. W. W. Cook (New Haven, Connecticut: Yale University Press, 1919).

10. Alasdair MacIntyre, *After Virtue* (Notre Dame, Indiana: University of Notre Dame Press, 1981), pp. 66–67; hereafter cited as AV.

11. Stating one of his reasons for this discomfort, Taylor says, "I'm unhappy with the term 'communitarianism'. It sounds as though the critics of . . . liberalism wanted to substitute some other all-embracing principle, which would in some equal and opposite way exalt the life of the community over everything. Really the aim (as far as I'm concerned) is more modest . . ." ("Reply [to Daniel M. Weinstock]," in *Philosophy in an Age of Pluralism: The Philosophy of Charles Taylor in Question*, ed. Tully, p. 250).

12. Charles Taylor, "Shared and Divergent Values" (1991), in *Reconciling the Solitudes: Essays on Canadian Federalism and Nationalism*, ed. Guy Laforest (Montreal and Kingston: McGill-Queens University Press, 1993), p. 165; hereafter cited as DV.

13. Zygmunt Bauman, *Freedom* (Minneapolis: University of Minnesota Press, 1988), p. 3.

14. What is central for MacIntyre, in this connection, is that these others can hold me accountable, and I can call them to account. Focally concerned with the self as moral agent, MacIntyre takes accountability and identity to be inseparable.

15. Charles Taylor, "The Politics of Recognition," in *Multiculturalism and "The Politics of Recognition": An Essay—With Commentary by Amy Gutman et al.* (Princeton, New Jersey: Princeton University Press, 1992), p. 25; hereafter cited as PRec. As he had earlier put it in an article on "The Political Intelligentsia: A Case Study" (1965), "the problem of identity" is "the problem of how individuals or members of a group see

themselves" (*Reconciling the Solitudes: Essays on Canadian Federalism and Nationalism*, ed. Guy Laforest [Montreal and Kingston: McGill-Queens University Press, 1993], p. 13).

16. Charles Taylor, "Why Do Nations Have to Become States?" (1979), in *Reconciling the Solitudes*, p. 45; hereafter cited as NS.

17. The fact that the sense of identity is formed in dialogue with others is the reason, Taylor holds, that people, both individually and collectively, find recognition, in the sense of respectful acknowledgment, to be so important. Misrecognition, by which I take him to mean contemptuous treatment and characterization, also affects one's sense of identity: "a person or group of people can suffer real damage, real distortion, if the people or society around them mirror back to them a confining or demeaning or contemptible picture of themselves" (PRec 25).

18. Justus Buchler, *Toward a General Theory of Human Judgment* (New York: Columbia University Press, 1951), pp. 39–40; hereafter cited as TGT.

19. Singer, *Operative Rights* (Albany: State University of New York Press, 1993).

20. Margaret MacDonald, "Natural Rights." *Proceedings of the Aristotelian Society* (1947–1948), repr. in *Theories of Rights*, ed. Jeremy Waldron (Oxford: Oxford University Press, 1989).

21. Rex Martin, *A System of Rights* (Oxford: Clarendon Press, 1993), p. l.

22. Hohfeld, *Fundamental Legal Conceptions*.

23. Virginia Held, *Rights and Goods: Justifying Social Action* (New York: The Free Press, 1984), p. 15.

24. Cf. Chapter 6 above.

25. This is a somewhat modified formulation of my original concept of generic rights as those that ought to be operative in all normative communities.

26. George Herbert Mead, *Mind, Self, and Society: From the Standpoint of a Social Behaviorist*, ed. Charles W. Morris (Chicago: The University of Chicago Press, 1934).

27. John Rawls, *A Theory of Justice* (Cambridge, Massachusetts: The Belknap Press of Harvard University Press, 1971), p. 515.

28. Joseph Raz, *The Morality of Freedom* (Oxford: Clarendon Press, 1986), p. 247. "It is a life which is here primarily judged as autonomous or not . . ." ibid., p. 371.

29. Ibid., pp. 370, 371.

30. I often use 'judgment' in the broad sense defined by Justus Buchler to encompass all the ways of making, saying, or doing. Cf. his *Toward a General Theory*, pp. 47–56. Here, my intent is somewhat narrower.

31. Cf. Chapter 8 above.

32. Quebec's Bill 101 specifies that Francophone parents must send their children to French-language schools, in order, as Taylor says, "to ensure the flourishing and survival of [the] community." While permitting Anglophone Canadians to send their children to English schools, the bill also requires immigrants to send their children to French schools, favoring French culture over English. But the point at issue here is whether Francophones (or the members of any cultural group) should be compelled to perpetuate their own language and culture rather than simply having the right to do so. Cf. "Shared and Divergent Values," pp. 166, 165, 173, 176; cf. PRec 52–61.

POSTSCRIPT

But I Have a Right!

I

SEVERAL REVIEWERS OF MY BOOK *Operative Rights* have made criticisms and raised questions that I believe deserve a response.[1] To make what I say intelligible to readers who may not have read that book, I shall supplement my answers with summaries of the features of my theory to which they seem to be reacting and illustrations of the way the principles involved can be applied. To begin with, I need to amplify a point I make in the book. I do not think that a theory of rights, by itself, is adequate as a basis for moral theory.[2] Moral issues do not all have to do with rights, and not all moral obligations rest on rights (the obligation to be charitable, which many of us accept, is an example). The obligation that I hold to be inseparable from any rights–entitlement is only one kind of moral obligation. Thus, I have not proposed a "rights-based morality" and, while I hope to do more work in the field, I cannot promise that I will ever develop a comprehensive moral theory. In my opinion, the most adequate approach to values and morality thus far is that of John Dewey.

In characterizing rights as social institutions rather than as inherent traits of essential human nature, I am rejecting the traditional concept of "natural rights," although I agree with George Herbert Mead that, as products of social interaction, rights are nevertheless natural in an everyday sense of this term.[3] In addition, by analyzing rights in terms of norms that confer specific entitlements and correlative obligations of respect for those entitlements, I have differentiated between rights and other kinds of moral obligation. Rex Martin, whose work *A System of Rights* I have already mentioned, takes a comparable position, saying, "Natural or human rights are not simply demands of morality, not even of distributive justice." In Martin's words, "Without . . . recognition and maintenance, whatever was said to be justified

on moral grounds would not be a proper human right."[4] He
quotes the British philosopher T. H. Green: "Rights are made by
recognition. There is no right but 'thinking makes it so. . . '."[5]
For Green's "thinking," I have substituted what Mead calls "the
attitude of a generalized other or community,"[6] and what Green
and Martin characterize as "recognition" I speak of as understanding and take to incorporate and be expressed in respect. That
is, on my view rights are "made by" society through the establishment of social norms, a process that occurs only in actual communities whose members evolve those norms and come to
internalize them as part of the process of acculturation. And I
insist that, in order for those members to "have" or participate in
rights, the norms that govern them must be maintained in operation—perpetuated—although not necessarily in unmodified
form. Since I see rights as ways in which the members of a community relate to and interact with one another, 'participate' is the
more accurate term. What we *have*, when rights are operative in
our community, are rights–entitlements together with obligations
to respect them. Where a right is operative, every member of the
community has both the entitlement and the correlative obligation that makes that entitlement a matter of right. Rights (ordinary language sanctions this usage for what are technically rights-
entitlements) and their correlative obligations are social imperatives; they must be mandated by a community's social norms.
Therefore, one who does not belong to a community in which a
given set of rights–norms is operative would, to use the vernacu-
lar, "not have" that right. (For simplicity's sake, in the pages that
follow, by 'community' I shall mean normative community unless
I specify otherwise.)

Whether or not they are formally defined or promulgated as
law, there are rights operative in every community, rights–norms
internalized by its members and by which they are expected to
(and generally do) govern their conduct toward one another, even
if the language of the community contains no name for "a right."
For instance, there is no such term in classical Chinese, and it is
widely held that in Confucian culture, which is authoritarian
rather than egalitarian, there are no rights.[7] But consider the
norms concerning the family: despite the hierarchical structure of
authority in the traditional, Confucian family, the fact that the

family as an institution is taken to be rooted in the cosmic order implies that all members of the community are both entitled to others' performance of their familial roles and, reciprocally, obligated to perform such roles. They enact both the entitlement and the obligation within the families into which they are born and those into which they marry. To put this in the terms that I have used: both the entitlement and the obligation are relevant to all members of the community. Each would have the same obligation to any other, were that other a member of his or her own family; that is, the obligation is applicable to them as family members. The fact that the culture confers both upon everyone in the community makes participation in one's family and the performance of the proper behavior toward one by the members of one's family what I call "rights-entitlements," and the entitlements and obligations taken together, "operative rights."

Part of the difference among cultures is that there are different rights operative or institutionalized in different societies. However, I have argued that there are some rights, which I call "generic rights," that ought to be operative in all societies, including two *fundamental* generic rights and others that are either presupposed or entailed by these. More conventional rights-theories, identified with the "natural rights," "social contract," or neo-Kantian schools, take certain rights, usually called either "natural" or "human" rights, to be possessed by all human beings, resting this attribution on some feature of their common human nature. This concept of universal human rights is so pervasive in Western society that, when a given right is not operative and the entitlement is not respected, a person who is not treated as one who has that entitlement and thinks that she or he ought to be is likely to object, "But I have a right!" Moreover, where something taken to be a universal human right is not operative, both ordinary citizens and scholars will say that this right has been violated. Commentators on my theory of rights, pointing out that to say "I have a right" is an important defense in cases when the entitlement in question is not honored and the claimant believes it ought to be, have charged that this defense would have no meaning in a community in which there is no such operative rights-entitlement. Critics have also pointed out that, on my view, even if it ought to be universally operative, if a right is not operative in a given community, we could not charge that it has been violated there.[8]

Could the claim to have a right (i.e., a rights-entitlement) when there is no such right operative in one's community have any meaning beyond the weaker claim that one ought to have it? I would have to say that, with regard to that particular community, it could not. But in terms of the theory of community in which my theory of rights is situated, it could have a different meaning for some of that community's members in virtue of their membership in other communities with different social norms. We all belong to many communities, many of these not localized and, in fact, having members who may never have interacted or communicated with one another. Nevertheless, the normative perspective in virtue of which individuals are members of, say, the English-speaking community, would enable any selection of them to communicate with one another. So would the perspective provided by the norms governing the game of chess. Each of these is what I call an *extended community*. Like those of any other normative community, its members can all expect one another to govern their communicative interaction in a particular sphere by the same set of social norms. Similarly, as I have written,

> there is an extended community of rights, whose members have all internalized the culture of rights—the general principles governing and exemplified by all rights-relations—and may even try to govern themselves by those norms, whether or not there are rights operative in the organized communities to which they belong. All the members of this community know or are expected to know (at least implicitly) what it is to have rights-entitlements; they recognize an obligation to respect them; and they know to expect and require others to respect both their own and one another's entitlements even if, in the organized communities to which they belong, those rights are denied them [OR 65].

A person who respects rights-entitlements and is ready to exercise them, expecting them to be respected in return, can, speaking as a member of this (extended) community, meaningfully make the claim, "I have a right!" To say so within the confines of a local community in which that right is not operative, however, is, first of all, to risk not being understood. To the extent that one is understood (as one would be by people who are familiar with the concept of rights even if they have not internalized the norms governing the right in question and do not respect any such entitlement), to make such a claim is also to invite vigorous denial. But, false as it is, the statement that one has a particular right that is actually inoperative, having prescriptive force (conveying the meaning that we ought to have it), can serve as a way of suggesting that everyone in that community ought to have and respect that entitlement. Also, if we imagine a community in which the language of rights is altogether absent and the concept not formally understood (even if rights exist as institutions and the practices they involve are customary), to claim to have what we would call a "right," whatever term one uses for it, and explain what one means by this, can serve to introduce the concept. This is in fact what happened when Western literature on rights began to be translated into Chinese.[9] In short, to say, "I have a right!" can be to use this expression as an instrument for initiating a process of social change.

The more problematic question is whether a right can be violated in or by a community in which it is not operative. I have charged, for instance, that certain communities violate not only the rights of some or all of their members, but also the rights that I hold to be fundamental and generic and that, by definition, ought to be operative in all communities whether or not they are, specifically, the rights of personal autonomy and personal authority. (The reader will recall that by 'autonomy' I mean self-direction, judging for oneself; by 'authority,' legitimacy and deserving to be taken seriously.) Can a community in which these or any other rights are not operative accurately be said to violate them?

To say that a particular right is not operative in a community is not only to say that its members do not recognize any obligation to respect the entitlement in question, but also to say that there is no such right there. If this is so, then even though that right is recognized in an extended community to which some of its members belong, within the local community nobody has a right of that kind that can be violated. In the case of a right that the speaker believes ought to be operative but that is not, the charge ought to be, not that the right is being violated, but that it is being *denied*, that the community does not grant any such entitlement. In charging that there are communities whose norms "violate" what I take to be the fundamental generic rights of some or all of their members, we could say that in the extended community of those who respect that right, the denial would be construed as a violation. Nevertheless, in the community in question, the charge should be that entitlements that they ought to have as a matter of right are being denied to those persons. My usage can be explained (though not justified) by the fact that anyone who has internalized and governs him- or herself by the norms of the extended community or a particular community in which that right is institutionalized will see the denial as a violation. Charging that an inoperative right has been violated, like claiming to have a right in a community in which one actually does not, is inaccurate and misleading; but it does reflect the perspective I am prescribing.

II

I have also argued that rights of autonomy and authority analogous to those I take to be the fundamental generic personal rights ought to be operative for communities in their relations to one another, that is, as members of more inclusive communities. I refer to these as "communal rights," distinguishing them from the "collective rights" that pertain, not to communities as such, but to their members, jointly or collectively. (An example of a communal right would be the right of a cultural community to exist; its members jointly can have the collective right to communicate with one another in their own language.) I argue that some communities, at least, are eligible for participation in communal rights-relations in the sense that they have the power to do so. For this, a community must be able to function agentially, that is, to generate communal judgments and govern its interactions with other communities by shared norms. Large communities can function as singular entities by means of a vote.

Accepting the view that normative communities are essential to human life, at least as we know it, I maintain, to begin with, that the exercise of autonomy and authority by all members of any group engaged in a common effort is essential to the establishment of norms to govern their joint activity and, hence, to the evolution and stability of normative communities. Because it is so important, the free exercise of personal autonomy and authority ought to be protected, and the way to accomplish this is to establish that freedom as a rights-entitlement, operative not only in every developed community, but also in any group of individuals attempting to regulate their collective behavior or their common enterprises in some effective way (who are, that is, in process of forming a normative community). If people are to be willing to cooperate with one another and to conform to principles and policies that others are helping (or have helped) to shape, they must have the security of knowing that their autonomy is not threatened and that they are accepted and respected as authoritative participants in collective decision making. Feeling that their autonomy and authority are threatened, they are likely to try to dominate and control one another rather than work cooperatively toward common ends. Failure of its members to respect one another's autonomy and authority can thus undermine even an established community and jeopardize its very existence, underscoring the need for these to be guaranteed as personal rights.

It is hardly necessary to search for arguments in support of the thesis that the existence and integrity of a normative community can be threatened from without as well as from within. Nationalist struggles throughout the world illustrate the way communities can weaken or even destroy one another. The war in Bosnia is not only over geographic boundaries and political independence; from the first, it has been in large measure a battle over whether the Bosnian Muslim community should have the right to survive. Under the prevailing nationalist leadership, each of the major ethnic communities has come to pose a threat to the others. In a separate essay I have argued that peace and stability could only be established among them by means of a dialogue (which would have to be initiated and supervised by a disinterested outside party) in which all were accepted as legitimate participants, and the purpose of which was for the citizens to determine for themselves the conditions of their future coexistence and the terms on which they would henceforth regulate their mutual relations.[10] To ensure this acceptance, it would have to be understood by all

the members of each of the communities involved that its autonomy and authority were guaranteed as rights, and that this meant
that all participants, regardless of ethnic identity or geographic
location, shared the same rights and had the same obligation to
respect them. These rights would have to be operative among the
communities as such as well as among their members, individually
and collectively; as personal, collective, and communal rights,
they would have to govern the entire peace-making process and
eventually become operative in and among whatever political
communities might be established as its outcome. The joint operation of these rights is what I call, using Drucilla Cornell's term,
"dialogic reciprocity." Even though in the book on rights I do
not use the term (as one reviewer perceptively noted), what I am
talking about is genuine participatory democracy.[11]

The thesis that the fundamental generic rights should be extended to communities presupposes that those communities
should have a right to exist, and I have advanced this as a general
thesis. But does this imply, as one reviewer has suggested it does,
that all normative communities must be preserved or that all such
communities that come into existence are necessary to satisfy the
requirement that the necessary conditions of human living be
protected?[12] Does the generalization that normative community
is a prerequisite of human life entail that every such community
is indispensable or morally justifiable? Are the members of a community not entitled to allow that community to go out of existence? Should they, or anyone else, be prohibited from making
the judgment that the community is one that should not be permitted to exist or to retain the norms that are operative within it
or in its relations with other communities or their members?

To begin with, it is not necessary for any rights, including those
I contend ought to be operative for all normative communities,
to be implemented in every case or at every point in the life of
every such community, whether this be a community of individuals or an inclusive community of communities (cf. OR 46–48).
Should conditions arise in which a prescribed rights-entitlement
can be exercised, in principle any member of the community
could choose to exercise it, and, if the community did, any member who was in a position to implement the obligation to respect
that entitlement ought to do so. Although in principle it is rele-

vant to all, the right is applicable only to those in a position to actualize it. But while anyone to whom it is applicable would be empowered to claim it, there is no necessary requirement to do so.[13] If there were, the act would be coerced and not a right at all. This applies to communities as well as to individual persons. Even if the right of all constituent communities (all cultural communities, for instance) to continue to exist is operative within an inclusive community, any subcommunity may voluntarily dissolve itself, merge with another community, or disintegrate as a result of inertia, without its autonomy or authority being curbed by others and without its right to existence being either violated or denied. To say that normative community is a necessary condition of human life is not to say that any particular community or selection of communities is so, let alone that all the communities that have ever come into existence are equally necessary.

But should every normative community that comes into existence and endures be allowed to continue in existence, or to do so unchanged? This is a moral issue, and a serious one. Under ordinary circumstances, that is, absent compelling moral reasons, we should accept the obligation to respect the entitlement in question. If a community's members, whether as their express purpose or simply through the way they conduct themselves, act so as to keep it alive, to interfere with them is to deny—or, where these rights are operative, to violate—the community's right to existence. However, there are communities whose entitlement to exist, given the ends they promote, some might wish to challenge on moral grounds. A community wholeheartedly and irrevocably committed to the extermination of another community or its members would present such a problem, and it would be easy to argue that it should be outlawed. Could such a step be justified? To begin with, we must not forget that in view of the ever-present possibility of conflict with other rights and other values, no right, however important, can be absolute or unconditional. We cannot, without reservation, respect the right of autonomy of a proven felon and we feel no compunction in limiting this autonomy by imposing a prison sentence. I have categorized the rights to autonomy and authority as generic (meaning that they ought to be operative in all communities) and, further, as fundamental (in the sense that they both presuppose and entail other rights that are thereby rendered generic). Neverthless, the generic right of normative communities to existence and to the perpetuation of their norms is no more absolute or unchallengeable than any other. At the same time, because it is (or ought to be) a right, the existence of any given community and its right to its own identity—the collective right of its members to perpetuate the norms by which they govern their common practices and shared activities—should be protected unless the danger it poses is publicly and convincingly demonstrated to be so great as to make it impossible to contain. If it has acted upon its commitment to do violence (as in the case of the subway terrorist group Aum Shinri-kyu in Japan), such a community has forfeited its right to exist, at least without instituting radical changes. Short of this, if such action appears to be a genuine potentiality, its right to continue in existence should be placed under scrutiny. But before any further steps are taken, the community in question should be given the opportunity to defend itself in dialogue between its own representatives and representatives of all the other members of the inclusive community, a dialogue in which the fundamental generic rights are carefully and consistently kept in operation.

We may also ask whether there are other circumstances under which the norms of a community (and, hence, its identity) should be open to challenge by the wider community. Similar principles apply to the right of identity as to the right of existence: Neither is unconditional. But only when a community has norms that are incompatible with those of the inclusive community, so that they cannot all be consistently implemented by one and the same person, or when they are adjudged seriously unjust, should its right to those norms be brought into question. And even then, any challenge should be made publicly and discussed in an open dialogue within the inclusive community in which all parties' autonomy and authority are equally respected. Moreover, the norms and rights of the inclusive community should be taken to be no more absolute or unchallengeable than those of its subcommunities.

One more question arises in this connection. Can only normative communities have rights? What about perspectival communities such as the community of women (which must be distinguished from organized women's groups)? As defined, rights that are operative in a community are relevant to all its members. I have argued that the right to be treated as equals is a corollary of the fundamental generic rights, so that women and members of other perspectival communities such as minorities or people with physical disabilities are no less entitled than anyone else to exercise all the rights that are operative—and no less obligated to respect them. Moreover, where the members of such a community require special protection in order to exercise any given right, such protection is instrumental in securing the right and should be considered part of that right. But insofar as these rights are individually and not collectively or communally exercised, they are personal rights, relevant and applicable to persons as individuals, not collective or communal ones.

III

If, for a right to exist, is for it to be operative or institutionalized in a community, its being so is the sufficient condition of its existence. I am sympathetic to the view of Jan Narveson, that there is no right except an *enforced* right.[14] However, I cannot endorse this view unconditionally. In the first place, we must ask what it means to enforce a right or, more properly, enforce the obligation to honor the entitlement that it establishes. I do not draw a hard and fast line between "human" or "moral" and "civil" or legal rights, since moral rights can be written into law, although they need not be. (Laws against deceptive practices, for instance, which are in effect only in selected communities, are codifications of the more widespread moral right—i.e., the entitlement—to be told the truth.) What I term operative rights could be classed as moral rights, although I have not used this terminology. But only if such right is also a right under the law is legal enforcement possible. Violating a legal right is a crime and enforcement a legal imperative; if the rights specified by law are operative in the community, government is an instrument for their enforcement as well as for their codification. However, while rights-legislation, at least in a democracy, usually reflects the attitude of the community, this may not be the case, and rights that are initially introduced by this means may or may not become operative. If they do not, enforcement of laws defining them as rights can be difficult. But unless and until an operative right is written into law, only pressure on the part of other community members can possibly induce people who would not otherwise do so to honor it in actual practice.

Ideally, all the members of a community in which there are operative rights-norms would have internalized these norms and would not only govern themselves by them voluntarily but would expect others to do so as well. That this ideal is never completely realized must be admitted. Habitual criminals aside, there can always be persons who are members of a community in virtue of sharing other elements in its normative perspective but who do not accept, or may never have internalized, particular norms; and even those who have internalized the operative rights-norms and who understand that those rights ought to be respected do not all respect them, and those who do may not always practice that respect. The case is no different for legal rights than it is for moral rights. Property rights are an example of the former: the thief understands that stealing is wrong. And even in a society such as ours, where the norms dictate that they ought to be, promises are not always kept, even by those who understand that we have a right to this. To the extent that the norms governing them are voluntarily implemented, however, both legal and so-called moral rights are secure and do not have to be overtly enforced.

On the other hand, whether the rights in question are legal or only moral, to the extent that the norms establishing them do not fully or effectively govern the conduct and the judgment of those to whom they are applicable, they have less normative force and are only weakly operative. For the same reason, they might be less likely to be enforceable. However, this is not the same as being inoperative—not being rights at all. From a Pragmatist point of view, should we say, when the force of the norms governing a right is weak, that there is no such right, or that there is an existent right that ought to be implemented? Or should we abandon the ontological dichotomy altogether and talk instead of degrees of normative force? The latter is what I would advocate (going beyond what is stated in the book).

Another aspect of this issue needs to be clarified as well. It would seem that in order for a right to be operative in a given social community, it must be agreed upon by every member of that community, each of whom must share "the attitude of the generalized other" that defines the community and must act accordingly.[15] The problem is that every social or geographic community, whether it be a political community such as a state or city or tribe, or an informally constituted community such as a neighborhood, is composed of a multiplicity of subcommunities, and the normative community in which any given set of rights-norms is operative may not encompass the inclusive community in its entirety. Yet, if a perspective or set of norms governing particular rights is predominant in the wider community, it is likely that the rights it defines are recognized (in the sense of being discriminated or identified) by all the latter's members. That is, even those who do not consider them to be rights, or who do not think they should be, are aware that, in the community at large, most people do take them to be so. I would say that, just as when the norms are imperfectly operative among those who nevertheless accept them, the smaller the proportion of those in a social community for whom rights–norms are actually operative, the weaker their normative force there.

Two questions have been raised about my position concerning persons who have lost the power to participate in rights on their own or have never developed it: First, is my argument adequate to *guarantee* rights for "comatose, brain-injured, and hopelessly imbecile human beings"? Second, even if it is, don't traditional theories grounding rights in human nature provide a *stronger* guarantee?[16] To begin with, the only guarantee I see for any rights is that provided by the norms that govern them, which is to say that it rests with society, the communities in which rights are operative. So-called "universal human rights," or "natural rights," in practice provide no other guarantee: If those rights are not operative in human communities, they can only be ideals, not actualities, and the concept of a universal (normative) community of rights is similarly ideal.[17] Treating rights as social institutions, I cannot accept the principle that human nature guarantees rights. Nevertheless, rights presuppose a distinctively human capacity, the capacity to internalize and govern oneself by rights-norms. Can one who has never had this capacity or who has lost it still "have rights"? Concerning the latter, if we take identity, as I contend we should, to be a function of continuity rather than of persistent sameness, we understand that a person retains his or her identity despite undergoing changes.[18] If that person ceases, through illness or injury, to be able to make the necessary judgments, it is this same person who is comatose or brain-injured. On these grounds I have argued that operative rights continue to be relevant and applicable to such persons despite the fact that they can be exercised only by their representatives. Even after death, when in ordinary language we would say a person no longer exists, it is that person who has died and whose having lived is still efficacious. Insofar as the person has lived in it, the world (the identity of which is also a function of continuity) differs from what it would be had she or he not done so. In Buchler's language, we would say that the person "prevails"—prevails now as dead even as she or he had prevailed as living.[19] Being the same person, she or he retains any rights that are applicable, an example being the entitlement to have one's will executed—an entitlement that persists until that process is completed. In exercising the claim to this entitlement, the executors of the will are expressing not only their own but also the testator's respect for the entitlement. This is because to understand an entitlement as a right, even with reference to oneself, is to apply to it the attitude of the generalized other in terms of which it is to be treated as such.

In addition to arguing that the comatose and the dead retain the rights in which they participated during their active lives, I have contended that those with only limited ability to participate actively in rights-relations should be counted eligible for rights and assisted, to the extent that this is necessary, in claiming and respecting rights-entitlements. A person with some capacity to understand what is entailed in having and respecting rights should be helped to understand when she or he should be or is in a position to exercise a rights-entitlement and also be helped, as far as possible, to fulfill the obligation to respect one when this is applicable, thus actualizing whatever potentialities that person has. To the extent that this is impossible, rights that are applicable can, again, be implemented through representation. A newborn, not yet having developed the capacity to judge and act in the ways called for by the institution of rights, is strictly not able—and, hence, should not be eligible—to participate in it. I have argued, however, that from birth infants should be treated *as if* they were participants in order to cultivate that capacity and instill the operative rights-norms and, of course, infants and small children can also be represented by adults in the implementation of rights. As in the case of the comatose or brain-injured, the principle of representation should also apply to a fetus that has reached the point at which it could survive outside the womb, on the grounds that a viable fetus must be assumed to have a potential capacity for participation in rights, a potentiality that, before reaching this stage of development, it lacked. I do not take rights to be relevant before this stage; other moral principles would have to apply. Regarding the few persons, however mature or immature, who are totally unable to develop the powers necessary to claim or respect or understand rights, I have contended that we can talk only of benefits, not of rights. One who is totally unable to comprehend what it means to have or to respect an entitlement, and for whom there is no hope of developing such understanding, will never be able to participate in rights. This does not mean, however, that I deny altogether the moral relevance of rights to such persons. I suggest a "principle of comparable or analogous benefit," which "would mean that, to the extent that they can benefit from being treated as if they had particular rights-entitlements, severely handicapped individuals should be so treated" (OR 44). I would now endorse this suggestion more strongly than I did in the book. Nevertheless, a benefit, even one that we are morally obligated to bestow, is not a right.

I do not claim that my theory provides as strong a formal guarantee of rights as a "natural rights" theory does. I find the latter guarantee to be empty, however, since, where the institution did not exist and the norms governing it were not operative, having rights would have no consequences and, in the Pragmatist sense of the term, no meaning. More important, I think, is the fact that I would not claim that I provide an equally strong guarantee of rights for all persons or all communities under any and all circumstances. As we are forced to acknowledge whenever it is necessary to adjudicate a conflict of rights, the weight to be given a right must be situationally determined. Similarly, rights do not inherently "trump" other values. Their implementation, like all human conduct, especially moral conduct, requires judgment. All judgment is situational or contextual and all judgment emanates from and is shaped by a perspective. Not only is the appraisal of a situation or context a judgment; adopting a perspective for judging also involves judgment, even though in many cases the judgment is not reflective or thoughtful but routine and mechanical.[20] Whether we would wish it to do so or not, I believe that the Peirceian principle of fallibilism necessarily applies. The best we can do is try to arrive at and justify our judgments as rationally as is in our power.

NOTES

1. Beth J. Singer, *Operative Rights* (Albany: State University of New York Press, 1993); hereafter cited as OR.

2. Cf. Joseph Betz's review of *Operative Rights* in *Journal of Speculative Philosophy*, 10, No. 2 (1996), 148–153.

3. See above, Chapter 8.

4. Rex Martin, *A System of Rights* (Oxford: Clarendon Press, 1993), p. 97. Richard E. Flathman also construes rights as social practices and provides a naturalistic explanation and justification of them. However, unlike my own view, Flathman's is individualistic, despite the fact that he insists that one can claim and exercise rights only within a society and polity of which one is a part. Cf. *The Practice of Rights* (Cambridge: Cambridge University Press, 1976), especially Chapter 9, "Rights and Community."

5. T. H. Green, *Lectures on the Principles of Political Obligation and Other Writings*, ed. Paul Harris and John Morrow (Cambridge: Cambridge University Press, 1968), p. 106. Cf. Chapter 3 above.

6. George Herbert Mead, *Mind, Self, and Society: From the Standpoint of a Social Behaviorist*, ed. Charles W. Morris (Chicago: The University of Chicago Press, 1934).

7. "In China . . . mainstream social and political thought has developed without a notion of individual rights, at least until the beginning of the twentieth century" (Julia Tao, "The Chinese Moral Ethos and the Concept of Individual Rights," *Journal of Applied Philosophy*, 7, No. 2 [1990], 119).

8. See, for example, the review by William J. Langenfus in *Philosophy and Social Criticism*, 21, No.1 (1995), 111–117.

9. After pointing out that "there was no word in the classical texts equivalent to 'rights'," Julia Tao tells us, citing as authority Professor

Wang Gunwu, vice chancellor of the University of Hong Kong, that in translating Western texts, "The word chosen for the abstract concept of rights was *ch'uan-li* which combines the character *ch'uan* meaning 'power', 'influence' and 'privilege' and *li* meaning 'profit' and 'benefits' " ("The Chinese Moral Ethos and the Concept of Individual Rights," 120).

10. "Nationalism and Dehostilization," an invited paper at the conference on "The United Nations at Fifty: (1945–1995): At the Threshold of a New World Order," held at Hofstra University, March 16–18, 1995. In view of the Dayton Accords, the proposal made in this essay, which was a specific one based upon a request from parties in Sarajevo for the establishment of what they called a United Nations Transitional Authority, is outdated, but especially in view of the difficulty of implementing the Accords, I think it still has relevance to the point I am trying to make here.

11. Cf. Betz's review.

12. See Langenfus's review cited in note 8, above.

13. One may also waive a right, which is a stronger step than simply omitting to claim it and would entail additional considerations.

14. Jan Narveson, "Pacifism: A Philosophical Analysis," *Ethics*, 78 (1968), quoted by Joseph Betz. Gábor Szabó, in his review of *Operative Rights*, calls attention to the role of the state in shaping as well as enforcing rights (*Magyar Filozofiai Szemle*, 5–6 [1995]). (In Hungarian; I am grateful to John Lachs for providing me with a translation.)

15. See Szabó's review.

16. See Betz's review of *Operative Rights*.

17. This is to say, in response to Szabó, that there is not and, I believe, cannot be, a universal "generalized other" (Szabó's review).

18. The theory of identity on which my own is based was developed by Justus Buchler in *Metaphysics of Natural Complexes* (1966); the second, expanded edition, was edited by Kathleen Wallace and Armen Marsoobian, with Robert S. Corrington (Buffalo: State University of New York Press, 1990). Cf. John Dewey, "The human individual is himself a history, a career . . ." ("Time and Individuality" *Time and Its Mysteries*, second series [New York: New York University Press, 1940]; repr. in *John Dewey: The Later Works*. XIV. *1939–1941*, ed. Jo Ann Boydston [Carbondale and Edwardsville: Southern Illinois University Press, 1991], p. 192).

19. Buchler, *Metaphysics of Natural Complexes*, Chapter 2, "Prevalence and Alescence."

20. See Beth J. Singer, "Basing 'Ought' on 'Is'," *Metaphilosophy*, 25, No.4 (October 1994), 304–315.

BIBLIOGRAPHY

Asch, Michael. *Home and Native Land: Aboriginal Rights and the Canadian Constitution.* Vancouver: University of British Columbia Press, 1993.

Bauman, Zygmunt. *Freedom.* Minneapolis: University of Minnesota Press, 1988.

Betz, Joseph. "George Herbert Mead on Human Rights." *Transactions of the Charles S. Peirce Society,* 10, No. 4 (Fall 1974), 199–223.

———. "John Dewey on Human Rights." *Transactions of the Charles S. Peirce Society,* 14, No. 1 (Winter 1978), 18–41.

———. Review of *Operative Rights* by Beth J. Singer. *Journal of Speculative Philosophy,* 10, No. 2 (1996), 148–153.

Blackstone, W. T. "Equality and Human Rights." *The Monist,* 52, No. 4 (October 1968), 616–639.

Boldt, Menno, and J. Anthony Long. "Tribal Traditions and European–Western Political Ideologies: The Dilemma of Canada's Native Indians." In *The Quest for Justice: Aboriginal Peoples and Aboriginal Rights.* Ed. Menno Boldt and J. Anthony Long, in association with Leroy Little Bear. Toronto: University of Toronto Press, 1985. Pp. 333–346.

Boxill, Bernard R. *Blacks and Social Justice.* Totowa, New Jersey: Rowman and Allanheld, 1984.

Buchler, Justus. *Metaphysics of Natural Complexes* (1966). Ed. Kathleen Wallace and Armen Marsoobian, with Robert S. Corrington. 2nd ed. Buffalo: State University of New York Press, 1990.

———. *Toward a General Theory of Human Judgment.* New York: Columbia University Press, 1951.

Cornell, Drucilla. "Two Lectures on the Normative Dimensions of Community in the Law. II. In Defense of Dialogic Reciprocity." *Tennessee Law Review,* 54 (1987), 335–343.

Crawford, James, ed. *The Rights of Peoples.* Oxford: Clarendon Press, 1988.

Descombes, Vincent. "Is There an Objective Spirit?" In *Philosophy in an Age of Pluralism: The Philosophy of Charles Taylor in Question.* Ed. James Tully. Cambridge: Cambridge University Press, 1994. Pp. 96–118.

Dewey, John. "Democracy and Educational Administration." In *Official Report of the Convention of the Department of Superintendence of the Na-*

tional Education Association (1937). In *John Dewey: The Later Works.* XI. *1935–1937.* Ed. Jo Ann Boydston. Carbondale and Edwardsville: Southern Illinois University Press, 1991. Pp. 217–225.

————. "Democracy Is Radical." *Common Sense,* 6 (January 1937), 10–11. In *John Dewey: The Later Works.* XI. *1935–1937.* Ed. Jo Ann Boydston. Carbondale and Edwardsville: Southern Illinois University Press, 1991. Pp. 296–299.

————. "Green's Theory of the Moral Motive." *Philosophical Review* (1892). In *John Dewey: The Early Works.* III. *1889–1892.* Ed. Jo Ann Boydston. Carbondale and Edwardsville: Southern Illinois University Press, 1969. Pp. 155–173.

————. *Individualism Old and New* (1930). In *John Dewey: The Later Works.* V. *1929–1930.* Ed. Jo Ann Boydston. Carbondale and Edwardsville: Southern Illinois University Press, 1988. Pp. 41–123.

————. *Lectures in China, 1919–1920.* Ed. and trans. Robert W. Clopton and Tuin-chen Ou. Honolulu: The University Press of Hawaii, 1973.

————. *Liberalism and Social Action* (1935). In *John Dewey: The Later Works.* XI. *1935–1937.* Ed. Jo Ann Boydston. Carbondale and Edwardsville: Southern Illinois University Press, 1991. Pp. 1–65.

————. "Liberty and Social Control." *Social Frontier,* 2 (November 1935), 41–42. In *John Dewey: The Later Works.* XI. 1935–1937. Ed. Jo Ann Boydston. Carbondale and Edwardsville: Southern Illinois University Press, 1991. Pp. 360–363.

————. *Outlines of a Critical Theory of Ethics.* In *John Dewey: The Early Works.* III. *1889–1892.* Ed. Jo An Boydston. Carbondale and Edwardsville: Southern Illinois University Press, 1988. Pp. 237–390.

————. "Philosophies of Freedom." In *Freedom in the Modern World.* Ed. Horace M. Kallen. New York: Coward-McCann, 1928. Pp. 236–271. In *John Dewey: The Later Works.* III. *1927–1928.* Ed. Jo Ann Boydston. Carbondale and Edwardsville: Southern Illinois University Press, 1988. Pp. 92–114.

————. "The Philosophy of Thomas Hill Green." *Andover Review,* 11 (1889). In *John Dewey: The Early Works.* III. *1889–1892.* Ed. Jo Ann Boydston. Carbondale and Edwardsville: Southern Illinois University Press, 1969. Pp. 14–35.

————. *The Public and Its Problems* (1927). In *John Dewey: The Later Works.* II. *1925–1927.* Ed. Jo Ann Boydston. Carbondale and Edwardsville: Southern Illinois University Press, 1988. Pp. 235–372.

————. "Time and Individuality." *Time and Its Mysteries, Second Series.* New York: New York University Press, 1940. Pp. 85–140. In *John Dewey: The Later Works.* XIV. *1939–1941.* Ed. Jo Ann Boydston.

Carbondale and Edwardsville: Southern Illinois University Press, 1991. Pp. 98–114.

Dewey, John, and James H. Tufts. *Ethics.* New York: Henry Holt and Co., 1908.

Dewey, John, and James H. Tufts. *Ethics.* 2nd ed. New York: Henry Holt and Co., 1932. In *John Dewey: The Later Works.* VII. *1932.* Ed. Jo Ann Boydston. Carbondale and Edwardsville: Southern Illinois University Press, 1989. Pp. 1–462.

Dworkin, Ronald. *A Matter of Principle.* Cambridge, Massachusetts: Harvard University Press, 1985.

Eisenstein, Zillah. *Hatreds: Racialized and Sexualized Conflicts in the Twenty-First Century.* New York: Routledge, 1996.

d'Entrèves, A. P. *Natural Law: An Historical Survey.* London: Hutchinson University Library, 1951. Repr. New York: Harper Torchbooks, 1965.

Ewin, R. E. *Liberty, Community, and Justice.* Totowa, New Jersey: Rowman & Littlefield, 1987.

Ezorsky, Gertrude. *Racism and Justice: The Case for Affirmative Action.* Ithaca, New York: Cornell University Press, 1991.

Feinberg, Joel. "The Nature and Value of Rights." In *Rights.* Ed. David Lyons. Belmont, California: Wadsworth, 1979.

———. "The Rights of Animals and Unborn Generations." In *Philosophy and Environmental Crisis.* Ed. William Blackstone. Athens: University of Georgia Press. 1974. Repr. in *Philosophical Issues in Human Rights: Theories and Applications.* Ed. Patricia H. Werhane, A. R. Gini, and David T. Ozar. New York: Random House, 1986. Pp. 164–173.

Flathman, Richard E. *The Practice of Rights.* Cambridge: Cambridge University Press, 1976.

Fuller, Lon. *Legal Fictions.* Stanford, California: Stanford University Press, 1967.

Gauthier, David. "The Liberal Individual." In *Communitarianism and Individualism.* Ed. Shlomo Avineri and Avner de-Shalit. Oxford: Oxford University Press, 1992. Pp. 151–164.

———. *Morals by Agreement.* Oxford: Oxford University Press, 1986.

Gewirth, Alan. *Human Rights: Essays on Justification and Applications.* Chicago: The University of Chicago Press, 1982.

Golding, Martin P. "Towards a Theory of Human Rights." *The Monist,* 52, No. 4 (October 1968), 521–549.

Green, Thomas Hill. *Lectures on the Principles of Political Obligation and Other Writings.* Ed. Paul Harris and John Morrow. Cambridge: Cambridge University Press, 1968.

Grotius, Hugo. *Laws of War and Peace.* Trans. F. W. Kelsey. The Classics of International Law 3. Washington, D.C.: Carnegie Endowment for International Peace, 1925.

Gutman, Amy. "Communitarian Critics of Liberalism." *Philosophy and Public Affairs*, 14, No. 3 (Summer, 1985), 308–325. Repr. in *Communitarianism and Individualism*. Ed. Shlomo Avineri and Avner de-Shalit. Oxford: Oxford University Press, 1992. Pp. 120–136.

Hart, H. L. A. "Are There Any Natural Rights?" *The Philosophical Review*, 64 (April 1955). Repr. in *Rights*. Ed. David Lyons. Belmont, California: Wadsworth, 1979.

Held, Virginia. *Rights and Goods: Justifying Social Action*. New York: The Free Press, 1984.

Hinchman, Lewis P. "The Origins of Human Rights: A Hegelian Perspective." *Western Political Quarterly*, 37, No. 1 (March 1984).

Hoekema, David A. *Rights and Wrongs: Coercion, Punishment, and the State*. Selinsgrove, Pennsylvania: Susquehanna University Press; London and Toronto: Associated University Presses, 1986.

Hohfeld, Wesley Newcomb. *Fundamental Legal Conceptions*. Ed. W. W. Cook. New Haven, Connecticut: Yale University Press, 1919.

Intractable Conflicts and Their Transformation. Ed. Louis Kriesberg, Terrell A. Northrup, and Stuart J. Thorson. Syracuse, New York: Syracuse University Press, 1989.

Isaacs, Harold R. *Idols of the Tribe: Group Identity and Political Change*. Cambridge, Massachusetts: Harvard University Press, 1989.

Ittinuar, Peter. "The Inuit Perspective on Aboriginal Rights." In *The Quest for Justice: Aboriginal Peoples and Aboriginal Rights*. Ed. Menno Boldt and J. Anthony Long, in association with Leroy Little Bear. Toronto: University of Toronto Press, 1985. Pp. 47–53.

James, William. *Essays in Religion and Morality*. The Works of William James. Ed. Frederick Burkhardt. Cambridge, Massachusetts: Harvard University Press, 1982.

———. "The Moral Equivalent of War." *McClure's Magazine* (August 1910); and *The Popular Science Monthly* (October 1910). Repr. in *Essays in Religion and Morality*. The Works of William James. Ed. Frederick Burkhardt. Cambridge, Massachusetts: Harvard University Press, 1982. Pp. 162–173.

Johnston, Darlene M. "Native Rights as Collective Rights: A Question of Group Self-Preservation." *Canadian Journal of Law and Jurisprudence*, 2, No. 1 (1989). Repr. in *The Rights of Minority Cultures*. Ed. Will Kymlicka. Oxford: Oxford University Press, 1995. Pp. 179–201.

Kymlicka, Will. *Liberalism, Community, and Culture*. Oxford: Clarendon Press, 1989.

———. *Multicultural Citizenship: A Liberal Theory of Minority Rights*. Oxford: Oxford University Press, 1995.

Langenfus, William J. Review of *Operative Rights* by Beth J. Singer. *Philosophy and Social Criticism*, 21, No. 1 (1995), 111–117.

Lee, Felicia R. "About New York." *The New York Times*, September 12, 1992.

Lijphart, Arend. *Democracy in Plural Societies*. New Haven, Connecticut: Yale University Press, 1977.

Locke, John. *Two Treatises of Government*. Ed. Peter Laslett. Cambridge: Cambridge University Press, 1963.

Lomasky, Loren. *Persons, Rights, and the Moral Community*. New York: Oxford University Press, 1987.

MacDonald, Margaret. "Natural Rights." *Proceedings of the Aristotelian Society* (1947–1948). Repr. in *Theories of Rights*. Ed. Jeremy Waldron. Oxford: Oxford University Press, 1989.

MacIntyre, Alasdair. *After Virtue*. Notre Dame, Indiana: University of Notre Dame Press, 1981.

Maritain, Jacques. *The Rights of Man and Nature* (1942). Trans. Doris C. Anson. New York: Harcourt, Brace, 1943.

Martin, Rex. *A System of Rights*. Oxford: Clarendon Press, 1993.

Matters of Life and Death: New Introductory Essays in Moral Philosophy. Ed. Tom Regan. 2nd ed. New York: Random House, 1986.

May, Larry. *The Morality of Groups*. Notre Dame, Indiana: Notre Dame University Press, 1989.

McChesney, Allan. "Aboriginal Communities, Aboriginal Rights, and the Human Rights System in Canada." In *Human Rights in Cross-Cultural Perspective: A Quest for Consensus*. Ed. Abdullah Ahmed An-Na'im. Philadelphia: University of Pennsylvania Press, 1992.

McCloskey, H. J. "Rights." *Philosophical Quarterly*, 15 (1965), 115–127.

Mead, George Herbert. *Mind, Self, and Society: From the Standpoint of a Social Behaviorist*. Ed. Charles W. Morris. Chicago: The University of Chicago Press, 1934.

———. *Movements of Thought in the Nineteenth Century*. Ed. Merritt H. Moore. Chicago: The University of Chicago Press, 1936.

———. "National-Mindedness and International Mindedness." *International Journal of Ethics*, 39 (1929), 392–407. Repr. in *George Herbert Mead: Selected Writings*. Ed. Andrew J. Reck. Indianapolis: Bobbs-Merrill, 1964. Pp. 355–370.

———. "Natural Rights and the Theory of the Political Institution." *The Journal of Philosophy, Psychology, and Scientific Methods*, 12 (1915), 141–155. Repr. in *George Herbert Mead: Selected Writings*. Ed. Andrew J. Reck. Indianapolis: Bobbs-Merrill, 1964. Pp. 150–170.

———. "The Psychology of Punitive Justice." *The American Journal of Sociology*, 23 (1917–1918), 577–602. Repr. in *George Herbert Mead:*

Selected Writings. Ed. Andrew J. Reck. Indianapolis: Bobbs-Merrill, 1964. Pp. 212–239.

———. *Selected Writings: George Herbert Mead.* Ed. Andrew J. Reck. Indianapolis, New York, and Kansas City: Bobbs-Merrill, 1964.

Merton, Robert K. "Contributions to the Theory of Reference Group Behavior." In *Continuities in Social Research: Studies in the Scope and Method of the American Soldier.* Ed. Robert K. Merton and Paul F. Lazarsfeld. Glencoe, Illinois: The Free Press, 1950. Pp. 40–105.

———. *Social Theory and Social Structure.* Rev. ed. Glencoe, Illinois: The Free Press, 1957.

Mill, John Stuart. *On Liberty* (1859). Ed. Elizabeth Rapaport. Indianapolis: Hackett, 1978.

———. *Utilitarianism* (1861). Ed. George Sher. Indianapolis: Hackett, 1979.

Miller, David. *Market, State, and Community.* Oxford: Clarendon Press, 1989.

The Morality of Abortion: Legal and Historical Perspectives. Ed. John T. Noonan, Jr. Cambridge, Massachusetts: Harvard University Press, 1970.

Multiculturalism and "The Politics of Recognition": An Essay—With Commentary by Amy Gutman et al. Princeton, New Jersey: Princeton University Press, 1992.

Narveson, Jan. "Pacifism: A Philosophical Analysis." *Ethics,* 78 (1968).

Noonan, John T., Jr. "An Almost Absolute Value in History." In *The Morality of Abortion: Legal and Historical Perspectives.* Ed. John T. Noonan, Jr. Cambridge, Massachusetts: Harvard University Press, 1970. Pp. 1–59. Excerpt in *Philosophical Issues in Human Rights: Theories and Applications.* Ed. Patricia H. Werhane, A. R. Gini, and David T. Ozar. New York: Random House, 1986. Pp. 29–32.

Northrup, Terrell A. "The Dynamic of Identity in Personal and Social Conflict." In *Intractable Conflicts and Their Transformation.* Ed. Louis Kriesberg, Terrell A. Northrup, and Stuart J. Thorson. Syracuse, New York: Syracuse University Press, 1989. Pp. 55–82.

Nozick, Robert. *Anarchy, State, and Utopia.* New York: Basic Books, 1974.

Philosophical Issues in Human Rights: Theories and Applications. Ed. Patricia H. Werhane, A. R. Gini, and David T. Ozar. New York: Random House, 1986.

Philosophy and the Reconstruction of Culture: Pragmatic Essays After Dewey. Ed. John J. Stuhr. Albany: State University of New York Press, 1993.

Philosophy in an Age of Pluralism: The Philosophy of Charles Taylor in Question. Ed. James Tully. Cambridge: Cambridge University Press, 1994.

Plain, Fred. "A Treatise on the Rights of the Aboriginal Peoples of the

Continent of North America." In *The Quest for Justice: Aboriginal Peoples and Aboriginal Rights*. Ed. Menno Boldt and J. Anthony Long, in association with Leroy Little Bear. Toronto: University of Toronto Press, 1985. Pp. 31–40.

Pluralism in Africa. Ed. Leo Kuper and M. G. Smith. Carleton Library Series 79. Toronto: McClellend and Stewart, 1969.

The Quest for Justice: Aboriginal Peoples and Aboriginal Rights. Ed. Menno Boldt and J. Anthony Long, in association with Leroy Little Bear. Toronto: University of Toronto Press, 1985.

Randall, John Herman, Jr. "Idealistic Social Philosophy and Bernard Bosanquet." *Philosophy and Phenomenological Research*, 26, No. 4 (June 1966). Repr. in John Herman Randall, Jr. *Philosophy After Darwin: Chapters for the Career of Philosophy, Volume III, and Other Essays*. Ed. Beth J. Singer. New York: Columbia University Press, 1977. Pp. 97–130.

Rawls, John. *A Theory of Justice*. Cambridge, Massachusetts: The Belknap Press of Harvard University Press, 1971.

Raz, Joseph. *The Morality of Freedom*. Oxford: Clarendon Press, 1986.

Readings in Ethical Theory. Ed. Wilfrid Sellars and John Hospers. New York: Appleton-Century-Crofts, 1952.

Regan, Tom. *All That Dwell Therein*. Berkeley and Los Angeles: University of California Press, 1982.

———. *The Case for Animal Rights*. Berkeley and Los Angeles: University of California Press, 1983.

The Rights of Minority Cultures. Ed. Will Kymlicka. Oxford: Oxford University Press, 1995.

Ross, Sir David. *The Right and the Good*. Oxford: Clarendon Press, 1930.

Rousseau, Jean-Jacques. *Contrat social* (First Version). In *Political Writings of Jean-Jacques Rousseau*. Ed. C. E. Vaughan. Cambridge: Cambridge University Press, 1915.

———. *Discourse on the Origin of Inequality* (1755). Trans. Donald A. Cress. Indianapolis: Hackett, 1962.

———. *Of the Social Contract, or, Principles of Political Right* (1762). Trans. Charles M. Sherover. New York: Harper & Row, 1984.

Royce, Josiah. *The Problem of Christianity*. 2 vols. New York: Macmillan, 1913.

Sabine, George H. *A History of Political Theory*. New York: Henry Holt and Co., 1950.

Sandel, Michael. "The Procedural Republic and the Unencumbered Self." *Political Theory*, 12 (1984), 81–96. Repr. in *Communitarianism and Individualism*. Ed. Schlomo Avineri and Avner de-Shalit. Oxford: Oxford University Press, 1992. Pp. 12–28.

Sanders, Douglas. "The Bill of Rights and Indian Status." *University of British Columbia Law Review*, 7, No. 1 (1965).

Schneider, Herbert W. "Dewey's Ethics, Part One." In *Guide to the Works of John Dewey*. Ed. Jo Ann Boydston. Carbondale and Edwardsville: Southern Illinois University Press, 1970.

Sigler, Jay A. *Minority Rights: A Comparative Analysis*. Westport, Connecticut: Greenwood, 1983.

Singer, Beth J. "Basing 'Ought' on 'Is'." *Metaphilosophy*, 25, No. 4 (October 1994), 304–315.

———. "Dewey's Concept of Community: A Critique." *Journal of the History of Philosophy*, 23, No. 4 (October 1985), 555–569.

———. *Operative Rights*. Albany: State University of New York Press, 1993.

Singer, Peter. *Animal Liberation*. New York: Avon Books, 1977.

———. "Animals and the Value of Life." In *Matters of Life and Death: New Introductory Essays in Moral Philosophy*. Ed. Tom Regan. 2nd ed. New York: Random House, 1986. Pp. 338–380.

Smith, M. G. "Some Developments in the Analytic Framework of Pluralism." In *Pluralism in Africa*. Ed. Leo Kuper and M. G. Smith. Carleton Library Series 79. Berkeley: University of California Press, 1969. Pp. 415–458.

Stuhr, John J. "Democracy as a Way of Life." In *Philosophy and the Reconstruction of Culture: Pragmatic Essays After Dewey*. Ed. John J. Stuhr. Albany: State University of New York Press, 1993. Pp. 37–57.

Tao, Julia. "The Chinese Moral Ethos and the Concept of Individual Rights." *Journal of Applied Philosophy*, 7, No. 2 (1990).

Taylor, Charles. "Atomism." In *Powers, Possessions, and Freedom*. Ed. Alkis Kontos. Toronto: University of Toronto Press, 1979. Excerpt in *Communitarianism and Individualism*. Ed. Shlomo Avineri and Avner de-Shalit. Oxford: Oxford University Press, 1992. Pp. 29–50.

———. "Institutions in National Life" (1988). *Reconciling the Solitudes: Essays on Canadian Federalism and Nationalism*. Ed. Guy Laforest. Montreal and Kingston: McGill-Queens University Press, 1993.

———. "The Political Intelligentsia: A Case Study" (1965). *Reconciling the Solitudes: Essays on Canadian Federalism and Nationalism*. Ed. Guy Laforest. Montreal and Kingston: McGill-Queens University Press, 1993.

———. "The Politics of Recognition." *Multiculturalism and "The Politics of Recognition": An Essay—With Commentary by Amy Gutman et al.* Princeton, New Jersey: Princeton University Press, 1992.

———. *Reconciling the Solitudes: Essays on Canadian Federalism and Nationalism*. Ed. Guy Laforest. Montreal and Kingston: McGill-Queens University Press, 1993.

———. "Reply" to Daniel M. Weinstock. In *Philosophy in an Age of Pluralism: The Philosophy of Charles Taylor in Question*. Ed. James Tully. Cambridge: Cambridge University Press, 1994. Pp. 249–253.

———. "Shared and Divergent Values" (1991). *Reconciling the Solitudes: Essays on Canadian Federalism and Nationalism*. Ed. Guy Laforest. Montreal and Kingston: McGill-Queens University Press, 1993.

———. "The Stakes of Constitutional Reform" (1990). *Reconciling the Solitudes: Essays on Canadian Federalism and Nationalism*. Ed. Guy Laforest. Montreal and Kingston: McGill-Queens University Press, 1993

———. "Why Do Nations Have to Become States?" (1979). *Reconciling the Solitudes: Essays on Canadian Federalism and Nationalism*. Ed. Guy LaForest. Montreal and Kingston: McGill-Queens University Press, 1993.

Tennant, Paul. "Aboriginal Rights and the Penner Report on Indian Self-Government." In *The Quest for Justice: Aboriginal Peoples and Aboriginal Rights*. Ed. Menno Boldt and J. Anthony Long, in association with Leroy Little Bear. Toronto: University of Toronto Press, 1985. Pp. 321–332.

Thomson, Judith Jarvis. *The Realm of Rights*. Cambridge, Massachusetts: Harvard University Press, 1990.

Triggs, Gillian. "The Rights of Peoples and Individual Rights: Conflict or Harmony?" In *The Rights of Peoples*. Ed. James Crawford. Oxford: Clarendon Press, 1988. Pp. 141–157.

Wright, Lawrence. "One Drop of Blood." *The New Yorker*, July 25, 1994, p. 50.

INDEX

aboriginal rights, Canadian concept, 105. *See also* minority rights of indigenous peoples

accountability, MacIntyre's view, 166 n. 14

acknowledgment of rights, as obligation, 25

actions, communities' ability to perform, 66–69

adversarialism (principle of traditional rights theories), 3, 14–19; rejection of, 32–34, 161–162

affirmative action (U.S.), 24–25, 40 n. 6; and special rights, 104

agency: capacity for, and relation to rights, 35; communal, 67

agential communities, 66–68, 82, 87

agential subcommunities, 68–69

Ahenakew, David, 109

alienation, and enforced conformity, 70

animal rights, question of, 13–14, 153

animals, and rudimentary norms, 156

antinationalists (Sarajevo), 92

a priorism (principle of traditional rights theories), 3, 6–11; rejection of, 28–32

Aristotle, 51, 97

Asch, Michael, 108, 109, 114, 116

Assembly of First Nations (Canada), 114

assimilation, 109; and indigenous peoples, 110

asymmetrical federalism (Taylor), 110–111

atomic individual, 146

atomism, Taylor's analysis of, 144

atomistic view of rights, 5–6, 43; rejection of (Mill), 50

attitude of generalized other (Mead), 17–19, 27, 32, 64, 82, 102, 136–

137, 157, 170, 181; and community, 37; relation to Rousseau's "general will," 129

attitude of positive toleration, and democracy (Dewey), 137–138

Aum Shinrikyu, 178

authority (fundamental generic right), 71, 158, 160; to act on behalf of community, 68; collective, right of, 74, 96; communal, definition, 160; as entitlement to respectful attention, 158; personal, right of, 30, 158, 173; respect for, 78

autonomous judgment, 159

autonomy (fundamental generic right), 71, 158, 158–160, 160–161; collective, definition, 160–161; collective, right of, 74, 96, 164; communal, definition, 161; communal, right of, 160–161, 164; definition, 159; moral (Neo-Kantian), 96; personal, right of, 30, 158, 173; respect for, 78

Balkan states, and European Community, 80 n. 12

Bauman, Zygmunt, 145

behavior, control of, 64

benefits: comparison to rights, 69, 183

Betz, Joseph, 138 n. 1

Bill 101 (Quebec), 164–165, 168 n. 32

Bill of Rights (U.S.), 93, 136

Blackstone, W. T., view of rights, 10

Boldt, Menno, 108, 109, 113

Bonavita, Edie, 80 n. 12

Bosnia, 175

Bosnian Muslim community, 175

Boxill, Bernard R., 40 n. 6

Buchler, Justus, 150–151, 182; concept of community, 82

ial, 87; as central to human life,
102–103; definition, 62, 82, 137,
148; and fundamental generic rights,
158; necessary conditions of, 69–70;
as prerequisite for human existence,
69, 156
normative or prescriptive principles, 7
"normative existence" (Gewirth), 9
normative force, loss of, 156
normative perspective, 64, 71, 137,
147–148; and Mead's attitude of
generalized other, 64
norms, *see* rights-norms, social norms
North and South Korea, 80 n. 12
Northrup, Terrell A., 79 n. 9
Nozick, Robert, 7
Nunavut (proposed jurisdiction of
Inuit), 115

obligation: to accept disagreement in
conflict resolution (dialogic reciprocity), 76; to respect rights-entitlements, 152; role in rights-
relation, 64
obligations, and rights (Dewey), 124
operative rights, 28, 33, 65, 68, 151–
152, 171; definition, 33, 171; of
communities, 68; relationship to
laws, 37, 68
operative rights-entitlement, denial of,
65
operative social norms, 152, 156. *See
also* rights-norms, social norms
orchestra, as example of group judgment and action, 66
"otherness": perspective of, 84–85;
overcoming, 89–90
ownership, concept of (Rousseau),
45–46

participation in social relations, as requirement for having rights, 14
participation, in rights-relations,
34–36
participatory democracy, genuine, 176
Peirce, Charles S., 157
peoples' rights, 16
personal authority, fundamental generic right of, 30, 158

personal autonomy, fundamental generic right of, 30, 158
personal identity: and community
148–151; definition of, 147; question of independence from society,
143–144; as social in origin (Taylor),
147
perspectival communities, and rights,
178–179
perspectival community, 61, 82, 86,
89, 148; and conflict resolution, 86;
definition, 61, 82; formation of, 89;
inclusive, 86
perspective: common, 148, 150–151;
of cultural community, 101–102; as
part of identity, 147–148; personal,
149–150
perspective of generalized other, *see* attitude of generalized other
"place," and indigenous rights, 114
Plain, Fred, 110
political status, of indigenous peoples,
107 n. 2
politics, as dialogue (Miller), 136; as
interest-aggregation (Miller), 135
positive toleration, attitude of, and democracy (Dewey), 137–138
powers, category of rights (Hohfeld),
152
pragmatism, 121–138. *See also* Dewey,
John; Mead, George Herbert
pragmatist theory of meaning (Mead),
129
prejudice, against immigrant groups,
92
prescriptive nature of rights, 26; Mac-
Donald's view of, 151
prescriptive or normative principles, 7
principles of traditional rights theories,
3–19; adversarialism, 14–19; a priorism, 6–11; essentialism, 11–14; individualism, 4–6; rejection of,
27–40. *See also individual principles*
privileges, contrasted with rights,
105–107, 152, 153
property: concept of (Rousseau), 45;
right to (Green), 52
protection of community, as commitment of communitarianism, 143
proto-humanism, 13